Contents

Spiced lentil & butternut squash soup

Prep:10 mins **Cook:**40 mins

Serves 4-6

Ingredients

- 2 tbsp olive oil
- 2 onions, finely chopped
- 2 garlic cloves, crushed
- ¼ tsp hot chilli powder
- 1 tbsp ras el hanout
- 1 butternut squash, peeled and cut into 2cm pieces
- 100g red lentils
- 1l hot vegetable stock
- 1 small bunch coriander, leaves chopped, plus extra to serve
- dukkah (see tip) and natural yogurt, to serve

Method

STEP 1

Heat the oil in a large flameproof casserole dish or saucepan over a medium-high heat. Fry the onions with a pinch of salt for 7 mins, or until softened and just caramelised. Add the garlic, chilli and ras el hanout, and cook for 1 min more.

STEP 2

Stir in the squash and lentils. Pour over the stock and season to taste. Bring to the boil, then reduce the heat to a simmer and cook, covered, for 25 mins or until the squash is soft. Blitz the soup with a stick blender until smooth, then season to taste. To freeze, leave to cool completely and transfer to large freezerproof bags.

STEP 3

Stir in the coriander leaves and ladle the soup into bowls. Serve topped with the dukkah, yogurt and extra coriander leaves.

Low-fat Spanish omelette

Prep:10 mins **Cook:**15 mins

Serves 1

Ingredients

- 180g sweet potato , peeled and cut into 2cm chunks
- 5ml olive oil
- 55g onion , sliced
- 140g red pepper , diced
- 1 garlic clove , grated
- 5 slices turkey bacon , sliced
- 1 rosemary sprig (optional)
- 5 eggs (1 whole egg and 4 egg whites)
- 2 handfuls green salad leaves
- 150g 0% fat Greek yogurt

Method

STEP 1

Heat oven to 180C/160C fan/gas 4. Heat the sweet potato chunks in the microwave for 3 mins, leave to rest for 2 mins, then heat again for a further 2 mins, by which time they should be cooked through and soft.

STEP 2

Meanwhile, heat the oil in a nonstick ovenproof frying pan over a medium-high heat. Add the onion, pepper, turkey, garlic and rosemary (if using), and cook for 2-3 mins. When the potatoes are ready, add them to the pan as well.

STEP 3

Beat the egg and egg whites together, then pour into the frying pan. Use a spatula to move the eggs around, scraping it up from the base, for 1-2 mins or until there is a good proportion of cooked egg in the pan and the ingredients are well mixed. Put the pan in the oven and heat until the egg is cooked through. Slide the omelette from the pan and enjoy with a side salad and a good dollop of yogurt.

Low-fat turkey bolognese

Prep:10 mins **Cook:**45 mins

Serves 4 - 6

Ingredients

- 400g lean turkey mince (choose breast instead of thigh mince if you can, as it has less fat)
- 2 tsp vegetable oil
- 1 large onion, chopped
- 1 large carrot, chopped
- 3 celery sticks, chopped
- 250g pack brown mushroom, finely chopped
- pinch of sugar
- 1 tbsp tomato purée
- 2 x 400g cans chopped tomato with garlic & herbs
- 400ml chicken stock, made from 1 low-sodium stock cube
- cooked wholemeal pasta and fresh basil leaves (optional), to serve

Method

STEP 1

Heat a large non-stick frying pan and dry-fry the turkey mince until browned. Tip onto a plate and set aside.

STEP 2

Add the oil and gently cook the onion, carrot and celery until softened, about 10 mins (add a splash of water if it starts to stick). Add the mushrooms and cook for a few mins, then add the sugar and tomato purée, and cook for 1 min more, stirring to stop it from sticking.

STEP 3

Add the tomatoes, turkey and stock with some seasoning. Simmer for at least 20 mins (or longer) until thickened. Serve with the pasta and fresh basil, if you have it.

Prawn tikka masala

Prep:10 mins **Cook:**30 mins

Serves 4

Ingredients

- 1 large onion , roughly chopped
- 1 thumb-sized piece ginger , peeled and grated
- 2 large garlic cloves
- 1 tbsp rapeseed oil
- 2-3 tbsp tikka curry paste
- 400g can chopped tomatoes
- 2 tbsp tomato purée
- ½ tbsp light brown soft sugar
- 3 cardamom pods , bashed
- 200g brown basmati rice
- 3 tbsp ground almonds
- 300g raw king prawns
- 1 tbsp double cream
- ½ bunch of coriander , roughly chopped
- naan breads , warmed, to serve (optional)

Method

STEP 1

Put the onion, ginger and garlic in a food processor and blitz to a smooth paste. Heat the oil in a large flameproof casserole dish or pan over a medium heat. Add the onion paste and fry for 8 mins or until lightly golden. Stir in the curry paste and fry for 1 min more. Add the tomatoes, tomato purée, sugar and cardamom pods. Bring to a simmer and cook, covered, for another 10 mins.

STEP 2

Cook the rice following pack instructions.

STEP 3

Scoop the cardamom out of the curry sauce and discard, then blitz with a hand blender, or in a clean food processor. Return to the pan, add the almonds and prawns, and cook for 5 mins. Season to taste and stir through the cream and coriander. Serve with the rice and naan breads, if you like.

Cheese-stuffed garlic dough balls with a tomato sauce dip

Prep:40 mins **Cook:**35 mins plus at least 2 hrs-2 hrs 30 mins proving

Makes 20 - 25

Ingredients

- 50g butter , cubed
- 300g strong white bread flour
- 7g sachet fast-action dried yeast
- 1 tbsp caster sugar
- 200g block mozzarella , cut into 1.5cm cubes
- 65g gruyère , coarsely grated (optional)

For the garlic butter

- 100g butter
- 2 garlic cloves , crushed
- 1 rosemary sprig, leaves picked and finely chopped

For the tomato sauce dip

- 1 tbsp olive oil , plus extra for the bowl and baking sheet
- 1 garlic clove , sliced
- 250g passata
- 1 tsp red wine vinegar
- 1 tsp caster sugar
- pinch of chilli flakes
- ½ small bunch of basil , torn, plus extra to serve

Method

STEP 1

Heat 175ml water in a saucepan until steaming, then add the butter. Remove from the heat and leave to cool until the mixture is just warm (it should not be hot). Combine the flour, yeast, sugar and 1 tsp salt in a large bowl or stand mixer. Add the cooled butter mixture, and mix to a soft dough using a wooden spoon or the mixer. Knead for 10 mins by hand (or 5 mins using a mixer) until the dough feels bouncy and smooth. Transfer to an oiled bowl and cover with a clean tea towel. Leave somewhere warm to rise for 1½-2 hrs, or until doubled in size. Alternatively, leave to prove in the fridge overnight.

STEP 2

Oil and line a baking sheet with baking parchment. Knock the air out of the dough, then knead again for several minutes. Flatten a small piece of dough (about 20g) into a disc, and put a cube of the mozzarella and a pinch of the gruyère into the middle of the disc. Enclose the cheeses with the dough, then roll into a ball. Transfer to the prepared baking sheet. Repeat with the remaining cheese and dough, placing the dough balls ½cm apart on the baking sheet – they should be just touching after proving. Cover with a clean tea towel and leave somewhere warm to rise for 30 mins.

STEP 3

Meanwhile, make the garlic butter. Melt the butter in a small pan over a low heat, then stir in the garlic and rosemary. Remove from the heat and set aside until needed. Heat the oven to 180C/160C fan/gas 4. Brush the risen dough balls with the garlic butter, then bake for 25-30 mins until the dough balls are cooked through and the middles are oozing.

STEP 4

While the dough balls are baking, make the tomato sauce dip. Heat the oil in a saucepan and fry the garlic for 30 seconds. Tip in the passata, vinegar, sugar and chilli flakes, and simmer for 10 mins until thickened. Season to taste and stir in the basil. Brush the warm dough balls with any remaining garlic butter, then serve with the tomato sauce dip on the side for dunking.

Amatriciana chicken traybake

Prep:15 mins **Cook:**1 hr

Serves 4

Ingredients

- 1 long red chilli
- 3 tbsp tomato purée

- 3 tbsp olive oil
- 3 garlic cloves
- 8 skinless chicken thighs
- 500g new potato
- 4 thyme sprigs
- 140g cubetti di pancetta (or smoked bacon lardons)
- 400g tomato, half cherry or baby plum, the rest is up to you - any larger ones halved
- green salad and bread, to serve (optional)

Method

STEP 1

Heat oven to 200C/180C fan/gas 6. Find a large roasting tin that will hold the chicken thighs and potatoes in a single layer. Halve the chilli, scrape out and discard the seeds if you don't like it too hot, and remove the stalk. Put in a small food processor or mini chopper with the tomato purée, olive oil and garlic. Whizz to a paste, then spread over the chicken. Add the chicken and potatoes to the tin with a good grinding of black pepper and some salt, then mix everything together well with your hands. Add the thyme and roast for 30 mins.

STEP 2

Stir in the pancetta and roast for 15 mins more, then add the tomatoes and roast for another 15 mins until the tomatoes have softened and the chicken is cooked. Serve straight from the pan and eat with a green salad and some bread, if you like, for mopping up the juices.

Vanilla panna cotta

Prep:10 mins **Cook:**5 mins plus chilling

Serves 4

Ingredients

- 2 ½ sheets gelatine
- 150ml milk
- 400ml double cream
- 60g caster sugar
- 1 vanilla pod, split lengthways
- fresh strawberries, to serve

- strawberry compote, to serve

Method

STEP 1

Add the sheets of gelatine to a bowl of cold water and soak for 5 mins.

STEP 2

Pour the milk and cream into a saucepan with the sugar and vanilla seeds (to scrape the seeds out of the pod, use the back of a knife). Stir to combine and bring to a simmer, then remove from the heat. Take the gelatine out of the cold water and squeeze out the excess, then add to the milk mixture. Stir until completely dissolved. Tip into four ramekins and place in the fridge to set for at least a couple of hours.

STEP 3

To serve, turn each ramekin upside-down onto a serving plate. If the panna cotta won't drop out, carefully dip the ramekin in a bowl of warm water to loosen it. Serve with a drizzle of strawberry compote and sliced fresh strawberries.

Fresh pasta

Prep:30 mins **Cook:**2 mins - 3 mins plus resting

Serves 8

Ingredients

- 300g '00' pasta flour, plus extra for dusting
- 2 eggs and 4 yolks, lightly beaten
- semolina flour, for dusting

Method

STEP 1

Put the flour in a food processor with ¾ of your egg mixture and a pinch of salt. Blitz to large crumbs – they should come together to form a dough when squeezed (if it feels a little dry gradually add a bit more egg). Tip the dough onto a lightly floured surface, knead for 1 min or until nice and smooth – don't worry if it's quite firm as it will soften when it rests. Cover with cling film and leave to rest for 30 mins.

STEP 2

Cut away ¼ of the dough (keep the rest covered with cling film) and feed it through the widest setting on your pasta machine. (If you don't have a machine, use a heavy rolling pin to roll the dough as thinly as possible.) Then fold into three, give the dough a quarter turn and feed through the pasta machine again. Repeat this process once more then continue to pass the dough through the machine, progressively narrowing the rollers, one notch at a time, until you have a smooth sheet of pasta. On the narrowest setting, feed the sheet through twice.

STEP 3

Cut as required to use for filled pastas like tortellini, or cut into lengths to make spaghetti, linguine, tagliatelle, or pappardelle. Then, dust in semolina flour and set aside, or hang until dry (an hour will be enough time.) Store in a sealed container in the fridge and use within a couple of days, or freeze for 1 month.

Aperol spritz

Prep:5 mins No cook

Serves 2

Ingredients

- ice
- 100ml Aperol
- 150ml prosecco
- soda, to top up

Method

STEP 1

Put a couple of cubes of ice into 2 glasses and add a 50 ml measure of Aperol to each. Divide the prosecco between the glasses and then top up with soda, if you like.

Tomato & courgette risotto

Prep:10 mins **Cook:**25 mins

Serves 2

Ingredients

- 2 tbsp olive oil
- 1 small onion , diced
- 2 garlic cloves , crushed
- ½ tsp coriander seeds , crushed
- 200g risotto rice
- 500ml vegetable stock
- 200g carton passata
- 12 cherry tomatoes , halved
- 2 courgettes , halved and sliced
- 2 tbsp mascarpone
- parmesan (or vegetarian alternative), grated, to serve

Method

STEP 1

Put1 tbsp of oil in a large pan over a medium heat. Add the onion and cook for 5-7 mins until softened. Add the garlic and coriander seeds and cook, stirring, for another 1 min. Stir in the risotto rice, coating it in the onion mixture. Gradually add 300ml of the vegetable stock, stirring until fully absorbed by the rice between each addition. Pour the passata into the risotto, cover and simmer for 10-15 mins. Stir occasionally and add more stock as needed.

STEP 2

Meanwhile, heat oven to 200C/180C fan/gas 6. Put the cherry tomatoes and courgettes in a roasting tin, keeping them separate, drizzle with 1 tbsp olive oil, season and roast for 10-12 mins until just tender.

STEP 3

Add the mascarpone and plenty of seasoning to the risotto. Stir until the rice is completely cooked and the risotto is creamy, about 5 mins more. Add the courgettes and stir to combine. Serve the risotto in bowls topped with the roasted tomatoes and some grated Parmesan.

Fettuccine alfredo

Prep:15 mins **Cook:**10 mins

Serves 2 - 3

Ingredients

- 227g tub clotted cream
- 25g butter (about 2 tbsp)
- 1 tsp cornflour
- 100g parmesan, grated
- freshly grated nutmeg
- 250g fresh fettuccine or tagliatelle
- snipped chives or chopped parsley, to serve (optional)

Method

STEP 1

In a medium saucepan, stir the clotted cream, butter and cornflour over a low-ish heat and bring to a low simmer. Turn off the heat and keep warm.

STEP 2

Meanwhile, put the cheese and nutmeg in a small bowl and add a good grinding of black pepper, then stir everything together (don't add any salt at this stage).

STEP 3

Put the pasta in another pan with 2 tsp salt, pour over some boiling water and cook following pack instructions (usually 3-4 mins). When cooked, scoop some of the cooking water into a heatproof jug or mug and drain the pasta, but not too thoroughly.

STEP 4

Add the pasta to the pan with the clotted cream mixture, then sprinkle over the cheese and gently fold everything together over a low heat using a rubber spatula. When combined, splash in 3 tbsp of the cooking water. At first, the pasta will look wet and sloppy: keep stirring until the water is absorbed and the sauce is glossy. Check the seasoning before transferring to heated bowls. Sprinkle over some chives or parsley, then serve immediately.

Vegan pizza Margherita

Prep:15 mins **Cook:**15 mins plus rising and proving

Makes 2 large or 4 small pizzas (serves 4)

Ingredients

For the pizza dough

- 500g strong white bread flour, plus extra for dusting
- 1 tsp dried yeast
- 1 tsp caster sugar
- 1 ½ tbsp olive oil, plus extra

For the tomato sauce

- 100ml passata
- 1 tbsp fresh basil, chopped (or 1/2 tsp dried oregano)
- 1 garlic clove, crushed

For the topping

- 200g vegan mozzarella-style cheese, grated
- 2 tomatoes, thinly sliced
- Fresh basil or oregano leaves, chilli oil and vegan parmesan to serve (optional)

Method

STEP 1

Put the flour, yeast and sugar in a large bowl. Measure 150ml of cold water and 150ml boiling water into a jug and mix them together – this will mean your water is a good temperature for the yeast. Add the oil and 1 tsp salt to the warm water then pour it over the flour. Stir well with a spoon then start to knead the mixture together in the bowl until it forms a soft and slightly sticky dough. If it's too dry add a splash of cold water.

STEP 2

Dust a little flour on the work surface and knead the dough for 10 mins. Put it back in the mixing bowl and cover with cling film greased with a few drops of olive oil. Leave to rise in a warm place for 1 hr or until doubled in size.

STEP 3

Heat oven to 220C/200C/gas 9 and put a baking sheet or pizza stone on the top shelf to heat up. Once the dough has risen, knock it back by punching it a couple of times with your fist then kneading it again on a floured surface. It should be springy and a lot less sticky. Set aside while you prepare the sauce.

STEP 4

Put all the ingredients for the tomato sauce together in a bowl, season with salt, pepper and a pinch of sugar if you like and mix well. Set aside until needed.

STEP 5

Divide the dough into 2 or 4 pieces (depending on whether you want to make large or small pizzas), shape into balls and flatten each piece out as thin as you can get it with a rolling pin or using your hands. Make sure the dough is well dusted with flour to stop it sticking. Dust another baking sheet with flour then put a pizza base on top – spread 4-5 tbsp of the tomato sauce on top and add some sliced tomatoes and grated vegan cheese. Drizzle with a little olive oil and bake in the oven on top of your preheated baking tray for 10-12 mins or until the base is puffed up and the vegan cheese has melted and is bubbling and golden in patches.

STEP 6

Repeat with the rest of the dough and topping. Serve the pizzas with fresh basil leaves or chilli oil if you like and sprinkle over vegan parmesan just after baking.

Lighter chicken cacciatore

Prep:15 mins **Cook:**50 mins

Serves 4

Ingredients

- 1 tbsp olive oil
- 3 slices prosciutto, fat removed, chopped
- 1 medium onion, chopped

- 2 garlic cloves, finely chopped
- 2 sage sprigs
- 2 rosemary sprigs
- 4 skinless chicken breasts (550g total weight), preferably organic
- 150ml dry white wine
- 400g can plum tomatoes in natural juice
- 1 tbsp tomato purée
- 225g chestnut mushrooms, quartered or halved if large
- small handful chopped flat-leaf parsley, to serve

Method

STEP 1

Heat the oil in a large non-stick frying pan. Tip in the prosciutto and fry for about 2 mins until crisp. Remove with a slotted spoon, letting any fat drain back into the pan, and set aside. Put the onion, garlic and herbs in the pan and fry for 3-4 mins.

STEP 2

Spread the onion out in the pan, then lay the chicken breasts on top. Season with pepper and fry for 5 mins over a medium heat, turning the chicken once, until starting to brown on both sides and the onion is caramelising on the bottom of the pan. Remove the chicken and set aside on a plate. Raise the heat, give it a quick stir and, when sizzling, pour in the wine and let it bubble for 2 mins to reduce slightly.

STEP 3

Lower the heat to medium, return the prosciutto to the pan, then stir in the tomatoes (breaking them up with your spoon), tomato purée and mushrooms. Spoon 4 tbsp of water into the empty tomato can, swirl it around, then pour it into the pan. Cover and simmer for 15-20 mins or until the sauce has thickened and reduced slightly, then return the chicken to the pan and cook, uncovered, for about 15 mins or until the chicken is cooked through. Season and scatter over the parsley to serve.

Mozzarella peppers with chunky Italian dressing

Prep:5 mins **Cook:**20 mins

Serves 2

Ingredients

- 2 red peppers
- 5 sundried tomatoes , in olive oil
- handful good-quality olives
- 85g can anchovy , in oil
- small bunch basil , leaves torn
- 2 x 125g balls buffalo mozzarella , drained and halved
- balsamic vinegar
- selection of antipasti

Method

STEP 1

Heat oven to 220C/fan 200C/gas 7. Cut the peppers in half, scoop out the seeds and white membranes with a spoon and discard. Drizzle the peppers with a little olive oil from the tomato jar, rub all over and season generously. Roast for 20 mins until softened and starting to char.

STEP 2

Roughly chop the tomatoes and olives, then mix in a small bowl with 2 tbsp oil from the jar. Cut 4 anchovies lengthways, giving 8 thin strips, then add to the bowl along with the basil leaves. Season with black pepper. Keep the rest of the anchovies in an airtight container in the fridge for up to a week.

STEP 3

Take the peppers out of the oven and turn the grill to High. Pour any juice out of the peppers, then spoon in a little of the olive mix. Snuggle a mozzarella half into each pepper and return to the roasting tin. Grill for about 3 mins until the top of the cheese has just softened, but not melted. Put the antipasti on a serving platter and add the peppers. Spoon over the rest of the olive mix and splash with a little balsamic vinegar. Enjoy with bread and a glass of wine.

Roast red wine lamb with Italian beans

Prep:15 mins **Cook:**1 hr and 30 mins Plus reducing time for the gravy

Serves 8

Ingredients

- 2kg leg of lamb
- 4 garlic cloves , sliced
- 8 good sprigs thyme
- 5 tbsp olive oil
- half a bottle red wine
- zest 1 lemon
- 1l hot lamb stock
- 3 red onions , each cut into 6 wedges
- 2 tbsp balsamic vinegar

For the beans

- 2 rosemary , needless roughly chopped
- 100g SunBlush tomato , drained and roughly chopped
- 3 x 400g cannellini beans
- handful flatleaf parsley , roughly chopped

Method

STEP 1

Using a sharp knife, cut small slashes all over the lamb, then push a slice of garlic into each. Put half the thyme, 3 tbsp olive oil, wine, lemon zest and a good grinding of black pepper into a large freezer bag. Addthe lamb, tie the bag tightly and refrigerate for at least 4 hrs, preferably overnight.

STEP 2

Heat oven to 220C/fan 200C/gas 7. Put the rest of the thyme into the bottom of a roasting tin then lift the lamb out of the marinade and sit on top of the thyme. Roast for 20 mins, then toss onions into the pan, drizzle with a little oil, then turn the oven down to 190C/fan 170C/gas 5. Roast for 15 mins/450g for medium. Meanwhile, strain the marinade into a pan, add most of the stock and boil until reduced by two thirds (this will take about 20 mins). Set aside. Gravy can be made ahead or the day before if necessary, as long as the meat has marinated for 4 hrs.

STEP 3

Once the lamb is ready, take out and rest on a board, wrapped in a tent of foil to keep warm. Set the onions aside in a bowl. Put the roasting tin onto a low heat and add the balsamic vinegar to the tin with a splash more stock and scrape all the meaty bits from the bottom. Tip into the jug with the gravy.

STEP 4

For the beans, add 2 tbsp oil to the roasting tin. Add the rosemary and tomatoes, and fry for 1 min until the rosemary smells aromatic. Tip in the beans, the red onions and the final splash of stock, then warm through. Season, then stir in the parsley just before serving. Serve on a platter, topped with the lamb.

Ultimate spaghetti carbonara recipe

Prep:15 mins - 20 mins **Cook:**15 mins

Serves 4

Ingredients

- 100g pancetta
- 50g pecorino cheese
- 50g parmesan
- 3 large eggs
- 350g spaghetti
- 2 plump garlic cloves, peeled and left whole
- 50g unsalted butter
- sea salt and freshly ground black pepper

Method

STEP 1

Put a large saucepan of water on to boil.

STEP 2

Finely chop the 100g pancetta, having first removed any rind. Finely grate 50g pecorino cheese and 50g parmesan and mix them together.

STEP 3

Beat the 3 large eggs in a medium bowl and season with a little freshly grated black pepper. Set everything aside.

STEP 4

Add 1 tsp salt to the boiling water, add 350g spaghetti and when the water comes back to the boil, cook at a constant simmer, covered, for 10 minutes or until al dente (just cooked).

STEP 5

Squash 2 peeled plump garlic cloves with the blade of a knife, just to bruise it.

STEP 6

While the spaghetti is cooking, fry the pancetta with the garlic. Drop 50g unsalted butter into a large frying pan or wok and, as soon as the butter has melted, tip in the pancetta and garlic.

STEP 7

Leave to cook on a medium heat for about 5 minutes, stirring often, until the pancetta is golden and crisp. The garlic has now imparted its flavour, so take it out with a slotted spoon and discard.

STEP 8

Keep the heat under the pancetta on low. When the pasta is ready, lift it from the water with a pasta fork or tongs and put it in the frying pan with the pancetta. Don't worry if a little water drops in the pan as well (you want this to happen) and don't throw the pasta water away yet.

STEP 9

Mix most of the cheese in with the eggs, keeping a small handful back for sprinkling over later.

STEP 10

Take the pan of spaghetti and pancetta off the heat. Now quickly pour in the eggs and cheese. Using the tongs or a long fork, lift up the spaghetti so it mixes easily with the egg mixture, which thickens but doesn't scramble, and everything is coated.

STEP 11

Add extra pasta cooking water to keep it saucy (several tablespoons should do it). You don't want it wet, just moist. Season with a little salt, if needed.

STEP 12

Use a long-pronged fork to twist the pasta on to the serving plate or bowl. Serve immediately with a little sprinkling of the remaining cheese and a grating of black pepper. If the dish does get a little dry before serving, splash in some more hot pasta water and the glossy sauciness will be revived.

Marmite & pancetta spaghetti

Prep: 5 mins **Cook:** 10 mins - 12 mins

Serves 4

Ingredients

- 500g pack of spaghetti
- 1 tbsp olive oil
- 200g pancetta , diced
- 80g butter , softened
- 2 tsp Marmite
- 50g cheddar , grated
- grated parmesan , to serve

Method

STEP 1

Bring a large pan of water to the boil and add the spaghetti. Meanwhile, heat the oil in a frying pan and cook the pancetta for 8-10 mins until crispy.

STEP 2

Once the pasta is cooked, drain, reserving a little pasta water. Tip the spaghetti back into the pan with the pasta water and add the pancetta with the fat from the pan, the butter, Marmite and cheeses. Use tongs to coat the spaghetti in the sauce and season with a little pepper. Taste and add a little more Marmite , if you like. Serve in bowls with extra Parmesan sprinkled over.

Next level tiramisu

Prep:35 mins **Cook:**5 mins plus 3 hrs chilling

Serves 6

Ingredients

- 3 egg yolks
- 100g golden caster sugar , plus extra for the dish
- 1 tsp vanilla extract
- whole nutmeg , for grating
- 150ml marsala
- 250g tub mascarpone
- 300ml double cream
- 200ml strong black coffee , cooled
- 24 sponge fingers or savoiardi biscuits

For the topping

- 100g golden caster sugar
- 1 tsp fine espresso powder
- 1 tsp cocoa powder , plus extra for serving

Method

STEP 1

Beat the egg yolks, sugar, the vanilla, a grating of nutmeg and 50ml of the marsala using an electric whisk in a heatproof bowl over a pan of barely simmering water for 10 mins, until pale and light. Put in the fridge to cool.

STEP 2

In a separate bowl, beat the mascarpone and cream together with an electric whisk until the mixture holds soft peaks. Gently fold the egg yolk and cream mixtures together with a spatula, being careful not to over-stir. Put the bowl back in the fridge to chill.

STEP 3

Scatter a little sugar over the base of a deep 20 x 20cm serving dish. Pour the coffee and the remaining 100ml marsala into a bowl. One by one, dip 12 biscuits in the coffee mixture on each side for a couple of seconds (don't leave them too long or they'll go soggy), then lay flat in the dish to cover the base. Spread over half the cream mixture. Dip the remaining biscuits in the coffee and arrange on top of the cream, then finish with a final layer of the cream. Cover the dish and chill for at least 3 hrs. Can be made up to two days in advance.

STEP 4

To make the crunchy topping, put the sugar and a splash of water in a saucepan, and stir to combine. Simmer over a medium heat until you have an amber-coloured caramel. Pour the caramel onto a parchment-lined baking tray and tilt to spread. While it's still hot, dust with the coffee and cocoa powder, then leave to set until hard. Break into small pieces, then blitz in a processor to a rough crumb. Sprinkle over the tiramisu and dust with a little cocoa powder to serve.

Sausage, sweet potato & sweetcorn bake

Prep:5 mins **Cook:**50 mins

Serves 4

Ingredients

- 2 tbsp rapeseed oil
- 300g sweet potatoes , peeled and cut into wedges
- 2 corn on the cob , each cut into 3
- pinch chilli or barbecue spices (use more if you all like spice)
- 12 chipolata sausages
- 1 tbsp grated parmesan
- barbecue sauce , to serve

Method

STEP 1

Heat oven to 200C/180C fan/gas 6. Put 1 tbsp oil in a bowl, tip in the wedges and toss them in the oil along with some seasoning. Arrange them in the centre of a large baking tray. Tip the corn into the bowl with the remaining oil and some seasoning, and arrange them on one side of the wedges. Sprinkle some chilli or spices on one half of the wedges (do the whole lot if everyone likes spices). Arrange the sausages on the empty third of the tray.

STEP 2

Put the tray in the oven and cook for 40 mins, turning the sausages and corn over halfway through. Take the tray out of the oven and sprinkle the parmesan over the corn, put it back in the oven and cook for 10 mins. Serve with the barbecue sauce.

Amarena cherry & almond tart

Prep:30 mins **Cook:**50 mins plus resting

Makes 12 slices

Ingredients

- 125g butter
- 125g golden caster sugar
- 225g plain flour
- ½ egg or 1 egg yolk

For the frangipane filling

- 125g butter , at room temperature
- 125g golden caster sugar
- 3 medium eggs
- 1 lemon , zested
- 125g finely ground almonds or almond flour
- 120g Fabbri amarena cherries (see tip)
- icing sugar , for dusting (optional)

Method

STEP 1

Mix together the butter, sugar, flour, a pinch of salt and the egg in a food processor to make a dough, then wrap and leave to rest in the fridge for 30 mins. The dough should be cold but still easy to work with by the time you roll it out.

STEP 2

Meanwhile, make the frangipane filling. Melt the butter in a pan over a low heat, then set aside to cool slightly. Beat the sugar with the eggs and lemon zest in a bowl until creamy. Pour in the melted butter while continuing to beat, then add the ground almonds (or almond flour) and fold into the mixture. Heat oven to 175C/155C fan/gas 3½.

STEP 3

Line a buttered tart tin or ring mould (approximately 23cm) with the rolled-out pastry dough, then trim any overhanging edges. Spread the frangipane evenly into the tin and arrange the cherries on top with some of their syrup, so the top of the tart is covered in a thin layer.

STEP 4

Put the tart in the oven and bake for about 40-45 mins until golden brown, puffed and firm to the touch. Leave to cool on a rack. Dust with some icing sugar, if you like, before serving in slices.

Italian chickpea stew

Prep:40 mins - 50 mins **Serves 8**

Ingredients

- 550g salad potato (such as Charlotte)
- 250g bag trimmed, washed spinach leaves
- 4 tbsp light olive oil
- 1 red onion , finely chopped
- 2 garlic cloves , finely chopped
- ½ tsp dried crushed chilli
- 200ml dry white wine (2 small glasses)
- 6 plum tomatoes , peeled, seeded and diced
- 2x cans chickpea (preferably organic), drained and rinsed
- 2 tbsp lemon juice
- 6 tbsp chopped fresh parsley
- 2 tbsp chopped fresh mint
- 4 tbsp extra-virgin olive oil

Method

STEP 1

Cook the potatoes in salted boiling water for 15-20 minutes until tender. Meanwhile, tip the spinach into a colander or sieve, pour boiling water over it from the kettle so the spinach wilts, then hold it under the cold tap until it's cooled down. Shake it well and leave to drain. Drain the potatoes and cut into 1cm dice.

STEP 2

Heat the light olive oil in a large pan and cook the onion and garlic over a low heat for 3-4 minutes until soft and translucent. Add the chillies and wine, tip in half the tomatoes and cook over a moderate heat until nearly all the wine has evaporated. Stir in the chickpeas, diced potatoes and spinach and cook for 5 minutes.

STEP 3

Add the lemon juice, parsley, mint, extra virgin olive oil and remaining tomatoes. Season with salt and pepper to taste. If the stew seems a little dry, add a splash of water or vegetable stock.

Italian apricot fool

Total time40 mins Takes 30-40 minutes, plus cooling

Serves 6

Ingredients

- 500g ripe fresh apricots , halved and stoned
- finely grated zest and juice of 1 lemon
- 140g golden caster sugar
- 3 tbsp Cointreau or other orange flavoured liqueur
- 500g carton mascarpone
- 142ml carton double cream
- 18 amaretti biscuits , plus extra to serve

Method

STEP 1

Put the apricot halves in a saucepan with the lemon zest and juice and the sugar. Shake the pan to combine, then simmer, uncovered, over a medium heat until the apricots are soft. This should take about 10-15 minutes.

STEP 2

Tip the contents of the pan into a blender or food processor and whizz to a purée. Decant into a bowl, stir in the liqueur and leave to cool – about 20-30 minutes.

STEP 3

Soften the mascarpone in its tub by whisking it vigorously with a fork. Whip the cream in a bowl – you want it softly whipped not stiff. Fold in the mascarpone with a large metal spoon, then lightly swirl in the apricot purée to make a pattern.

STEP 4

Spoon the mixture into six wine glasses. (At this point, they'll keep in the fridge for up to a day.) To serve, crumble over the amaretti, with a few on the side for dunking.

Mushroom & spinach risotto

Prep:50 mins - 55 mins **Serves 2**

Ingredients

- 1 tbsp olive oil
- 25g butter
- 1 onion, chopped
- 140g chestnut mushrooms, sliced
- 1 fat garlic clove, crushed
- 140g arborio rice
- 150ml dry white wine
- 4 sundried tomatoes, chopped
- 500ml hot vegetable stock
- 2 tbsp chopped fresh parsley
- 25g parmesan or vegetarian alternative, freshly grated
- 100g fresh young leaf spinach, washed if necessary
- warm ciabatta and green salad, to serve

Method

STEP 1

Heat the oil and butter in a large deep frying pan. Add the onion and cook gently for 5 minutes until softened. Stir in the mushrooms and garlic and cook gently for 2-3 minutes.

STEP 2

Stir in the rice to coat with the onion and mushroom mixture. Pour in the wine and cook over a moderate heat for about 3 minutes, stirring from time to time, until the wine is absorbed.

STEP 3

Reduce to a gentle heat. Add the tomatoes and 125ml/ 4fl oz of the stock and cook for about 5 minutes until the liquid is absorbed. Pour in a further 125ml/4fl oz stock and continue cooking until absorbed. Repeat with the remaining stock, until it is all absorbed and the rice is creamy and tender.

STEP 4

Stir in the parsley and half the parmesan. Season to taste. Scatter the spinach over the risotto. Cover and cook gently for 4-5 minutes until the spinach has just wilted. Serve immediately sprinkled with the remaining parmesan.

Gluten-free pizza dough

Prep:20 mins **Serves 4**

Ingredients

- 400g gluten-free bread flour
- 2 heaped tsp golden caster sugar
- 2 tsp gluten-free baking powder
- 1 tsp fine salt
- 1 heaped tsp xanthan gum
- 5 tbsp olive oil

Method

STEP 1

Mix the flour, sugar, baking powder, salt and xanthan gum in a large mixing bowl. Make a well in the centre and pour in 250ml warm water and the olive oil. Combine quickly with your hands, to create a thick, wet, paste-like texture, adding an extra 20ml warm water if the dough feels a little dry. Store in an airtight container or covered bowl in the fridge for up to 24 hours before using.

Salted caramel pear cake

Prep:1 hr **Cook:**50 mins

Serves 12

Ingredients

- 2cm piece ginger , grated
- 4 Williams pears , 3 grated over a sieve, reserving the pear juice for the caramel, 1 peeled, cored and chopped (do this when about to decorate)
- 360g self-raising flour
- 15g rye flour
- 1 tsp ground ginger
- ½ tsp turmeric
- ½ tsp nutmeg
- ½ tsp ground cardamom
- ½ tsp cinnamon
- 1 tsp baking powder
- 4 eggs
- 200g golden caster sugar
- 150g light brown muscovado sugar , sieved
- 150ml rapeseed or vegetable oil
- 120g natural yogurt
- toasted buckwheat , dehydrated pear and rosemary, to serve (optional)

For the pear-salted caramel

- 50g unsalted butter , plus extra for the tins
- 50ml reserved pear juice
- 150ml perry
- 100g light brown muscovado sugar
- 1 tbsp double cream
- generous pinch sea salt

For the icing

- 4 egg whites
- 250g golden caster sugar
- 250g butter , at room temperature
- 2 tbsp tahini
- 1 tbsp vanilla bean paste

Method

STEP 1

Heat oven to 195C/175C fan/gas 5 ½. Butter and line the base of three 20cm round cake tins. Add the grated ginger to the grated pear and push down with a wooden spoon to squeeze out as much juice as possible.

STEP 2

Mix the flours, spices, baking powder and 1 tsp salt in a bowl. In a stand mixer, vigorously whisk the eggs and sugars for 3 mins until thick and frothy. Slowly pour in the oil in a steady stream. Turn the speed down, then add the flour mixture, 2 tbsp at a time, alternating with the yogurt, until incorporated. Mix in the grated pear (for no longer than 20 secs). Divide the mixture between the tins and bake for 25-30 mins or until a skewer inserted comes out dry.

STEP 3

For the caramel, heat the pear juice and perry in a pan until reduced to about 50ml. Add the sugar and butter and whisk to a smooth caramel, then add the cream and whisk again until smooth. Add sea salt to your taste – I'd go for a generous pinch, so that the caramel is still fruity and sharp but has a little saltiness to it – then allow to cool slightly to just warmer than room temperature.

STEP 4

To make the buttercream, put the egg whites and sugar in the bowl of a stand mixer. Place the bowl over a pan of boiling water, then whisk until the sugar dissolves and the mixture is no longer gritty. Put the bowl in the mixer, then whisk until soft peaks form and the bowl returns to room temperature. Switch to the paddle attachment, then add the butter, one spoonful at a time. Add the tahini, vanilla and a pinch of salt, and beat to a light, fluffy icing.

STEP 5

Place the bottom layer of sponge on a platter or cake stand, then top with a layer of the buttercream and scatter over a third of the chopped pear. Repeat with the next two layers. To ice the cake, do an intial layer all over, chill in the fridge for 20 mins, then use the remaining icing to cover everything. Use a stepped spatula to spread it out evenly. Pour the caramel over the top of the cake, and allow it to drip down the sides. Scatter with toasted buckwheat, dehydrated pear and rosemary, if you like.

Pesto & goat's cheese risotto

Prep:2 mins **Cook:**30 mins

Serves 2

Ingredients

- olive oil , for frying
- 200g risotto rice
- 700ml chicken stock or vegetable stock
- 1 tub fresh pesto
- 100g soft goat's cheese

Method

STEP 1

Pour a glug of olive oil into a large saucepan. Tip in the rice and fry for 1 min. Add half the stock and cook until absorbed. Add the remaining stock, a ladle at a time, and cook until the rice is al dente, stirring continually, for 20-25 mins.

STEP 2

Stir through the pesto and half the goat's cheese. Serve topped with the remaining cheese.

Tagliata & borlotti beans

Prep:15 mins **Cook:**5 mins

Serves 2

Ingredients

- small bunch parsley
- ½ small bunch basil
- 1 small garlic clove
- 3 tbsp olive oil , plus a drizzle
- 1 tbsp red wine vinegar
- 250g rump steak , about 2cm thick
- 400g can borlotti beans , drained and rinsed
- 50g rocket
- 80g cherry tomatoes , halved
- 25g parmesan , shaved (optional)

Method

STEP 1

Put the parsley, basil, garlic, olive oil and 1 tbsp water in the small bowl of a food processor and whizz until the herbs are finely chopped. Transfer to a bowl, stir through the vinegar and season to taste.

STEP 2

Season the steak generously. Heat a griddle pan or non-stick frying pan over a high heat. Drizzle a little extra oil over the steak and fry for 5 mins, turning every minute. Put on a plate, cover and leave for about 5 mins to rest.

STEP 3

Toss the beans, rocket and cherry tomatoes in the herb mixture. Slice the steak into strips. Divide the salad between two plates, top with the steak and scatter over the shaved parmesan, if you like.

Baci di dama

Prep:15 mins **Cook:**20 mins Plus chilling and setting

Makes 16 biscuits

Ingredients

- 100g blanched hazelnuts , toasted
- 100g butter

- 100g caster sugar
- 100g flour (preferably '00' flour)

For the filling

- 100g dark chocolate , broken into small pieces

Method

STEP 1

Blitz the hazelnuts to fine crumbs, but be careful not to over-blitz – you don't want them to become oily. Add the butter and sugar, and blitz again until really creamy, then tip the mixture into a bowl and sift in the flour. Mix with your hands, then chill in the fridge for an hour or until firm enough to roll.

STEP 2

Heat oven to 180C/160C fan/gas 4 and line a large baking sheet with baking parchment. Tear off teaspoon-sized chunks of mixture and roll into balls, then place on the lined sheet around 2 cm apart. Bake for 15 mins until golden brown, then transfer to a wire rack to cool.

STEP 3

To make the filling, heat the chocolate in a bowl in the microwave, stirring every 10 secs until fully melted. Spread a small spoonful of chocolate on half the cooled biscuits. Leave to set for 15 mins then sandwich the remaining biscuits on top. Leave the baci di dama to set completely (put them in the fridge if the kitchen is warm). Serve with coffee.

Mozzarella, pepper & aubergine calzone

Prep:15 mins **Cook:**35 mins

Serves 4

Ingredients

- 400g strong wholewheat bread flour , plus extra for dusting
- ⅛ tsp salt (optional)
- 7g sachet fast-action dried yeast

- 2 tsp rapeseed oil , plus extra for the baking sheet

For the filling

- 2 tsp rapeseed oil
- 1 red and 1 yellow pepper , deseeded and cut into small chunks
- 1 large aubergine , halved lengthways and thinly sliced
- 2 large garlic cloves , finely chopped
- 1 tbsp tomato purée
- 1 tbsp balsamic vinegar
- small bunch basil , roughly torn
- 8 pitted Kalamata olives , halved
- 125g ball mozzarella (drained weight), quartered
- milk or beaten egg, for brushing

Method

STEP 1

Put the flour, salt (if using), yeast, oil and 300ml lukewarm water in a bowl and mix until soft. Knead into a ball (try not to add any extra flour) – it will be sticky but the flour will absorb some moisture. Return to the bowl, cover and leave somewhere warm.

STEP 2

Meanwhile, make the filling. Heat the oil in a large non-stick pan, then stir-fry the peppers for about 1 min until they start to soften. Add the aubergine and garlic and continue to cook over a medium heat for 8-10 mins, gently pressing the veg with a wooden spoon until it breaks down a little. If it doesn't, fry, covered, for a few extra mins.

STEP 3

Stir in the tomato purée, vinegar and 2 tbsp water. When the veg is soft, remove the pan from the heat and stir through the basil.

STEP 4

Heat the oven to 220C/200C fan/gas 7. Quarter the risen dough and roll each piece out to a 20cm circle on a lightly floured surface. Spoon a quarter of the filling over one side, scatter over a quarter of the olives, top with a quarter of the cheese, and brush the edges with the milk or beaten egg. Fold the dough over the filling and pinch the edges together at the side, a bit like making a Cornish pasty. Lift onto a lightly oiled baking sheet and brush with more milk or beaten egg. Repeat with the remaining dough and filling to make four calzones, then bake for 15-20 mins until golden. Leave to cool slightly and serve at room temperature.

Creamy courgette risotto

Prep:20 mins **Cook:**35 mins

Serves 3 - 4

Ingredients

- 50g butter, plus 2 knobs more
- 1 small onion, finely chopped
- 250g courgette, 140g coarsely grated, the rest diced
- 175g risotto rice
- zest and juice 1 lemon
- 1.2l vegetable (or chicken) stock, kept hot on a low heat
- 25g parmesan (or vegetarian alternative), grated
- 2 heaped tbsp mascarpone
- splash of olive oil
- 1 heaped tbsp toasted pine nuts

Method

STEP 1

Melt the butter in a sturdy frying pan, add the onion and gently fry until softened. Stir in the grated courgettes and rice, increase the heat and sizzle while stirring for 1-2 mins.

STEP 2

Add the lemon juice and a ladle of hot stock, and bubble over a medium-high heat while stirring constantly. When the liquid has just about been absorbed, add another ladleful of stock. Keep cooking like this for 20-25 mins until the rice is just tender and is creamy. Stir in the Parmesan, mascarpone and some seasoning, cover with a lid or baking sheet, and set aside for 5 mins while you cook the remaining courgettes.

STEP 3

Heat the remaining butter and a splash of oil in a small frying pan. Add the diced courgettes, and fry over a high heat for 2-3 mins until golden and just softened. Divide the risotto between shallow bowls or plates, then scatter with the diced courgettes and any buttery juices, the pine nuts and a few pinches of lemon zest.

Italian-style bass

Prep:6 mins - 10 mins **Cook:**15 mins

Serves 6

Ingredients

- 750g waxy potato , such as Charlotte
- 6 sea bass fillets, skin on, 175-200g each
- 250g pack cherry tomato
- handful black Italian olives
- 4-5 tbsp fish stock (preferably from the chiller cabinet)
- 4-5 tbsp dry white wine
- basil , to serve

Method

STEP 1

Heat oven to 190C/fan 170/gas 5. Slice the potatoes and boil for 6-8 mins until just tender, then drain.

STEP 2

Butter or oil one large or two smaller shallow ovenproof dishes that will fit the fish fillets in one layer (a couple of roasting tins would work well). Scatter the potatoes over the base of the dishes, then halve the tomatoes and scatter on top, along with the olives. Set the fish fillets among the other ingredients then pour over the stock and wine, then season to taste.

STEP 3

Cover the dishes with foil and seal the edges. Bake for 15 mins until the fish is tender. Serve each portion on warm plates and scatter with basil.

Winter panzanella

Prep:15 mins **Cook:**45 mins

Serves 4

Ingredients

- 1 cauliflower , broken into florets
- 100ml extra virgin olive oil
- 250g good bread, such as sourdough or ciabatta
- 2 red chillies , halved, deseeded and finely chopped
- 4 garlic cloves , finely sliced
- 8 anchovies , finely chopped
- 35g raisins , soaked in just-boiled water and drained
- 1 tbsp capers , rinsed of salt or brine
- 4 tbsp roughly chopped flat leaf parsley
- 5 radishes (preferably French breakfast radishes), finely sliced
- 1 tsp white balsamic vinegar or white wine vinegar
- juice of ½-1 lemon

Method

STEP 1

Steam the cauliflower until it's just tender (be careful not to overcook it), then set aside.

STEP 2

Tear the bread into small chunks and heat 3 tbsp of the olive oil in a large frying pan. Fry the bread over a medium heat (in batches if it's easier) until it's golden all over – each batch will take about 4-5 mins to get a good colour. Put all the bread back into the pan and add the chilli, garlic and anchovies to the pan (with another tablespoon of oil if necessary) and sauté for a further 2 mins, making sure the garlic doesn't get too dark. It should be golden, not brown. Tip the bread mixture into a broad shallow serving bowl and add the raisins, capers and parsley.

STEP 3

Add the rest of the olive oil to the frying pan and, over a high heat, fry the cauliflower until tinged with gold. You want a really good colour. Put the cauliflower in the bowl with the bread mixture, add the radishes, balsamic vinegar and the juice of ½ lemon and toss everything together. Season, but be careful about how much salt you use because of the anchovies. Taste to see if you need more lemon juice, or even more olive oil, and serve warm.

Roasted vegetable lasagne

Prep:25 mins **Cook:**1 hr and 10 mins

Serves 6

Ingredients

- 3 red peppers, cut into large chunks
- 2 aubergines, cut into ½ cm thick slices
- 8 tbsp olive oil, plus extra for the dish
- ½ quantity tomato sauce (see below)
- 300g fresh lasagne sheets
- ½ quantity white sauce (see below)
- 125g ball mozzarella (or vegetarian alternative)
- handful of cherry tomatoes, halved

Method

STEP 1

Heat the oven to 200C/180C fan/gas 6. Lightly oil two large baking trays and add the peppers and aubergines. Toss with the olive oil, season well, then roast for 25 mins until lightly browned.

STEP 2

Reduce the oven to 180C/160C fan/gas 4. Lightly oil a 30 x 20cm ovenproof dish. Arrange a layer of the vegetables on the bottom, then pour over a third of the tomato sauce. Top with a layer of lasagne sheets, then drizzle over a quarter of the white sauce. Repeat until you have three layers of pasta.

STEP 3

Spoon the remaining white sauce over the pasta, making sure the whole surface is covered. Scatter over the mozzarella and cherry tomatoes. Bake for 45 mins until bubbling and golden.

Cheat's aubergine Parmigiana

Cook:55 mins - 1 hr and 2 mins **Serves 2**

Ingredients

- 2 medium aubergines
- 400g can chopped tomatoes
- 2 x 125g balls buffalo mozzarella
- 30g grated parmesan (or vegetarian alternative)

Method

STEP 1

Heat oven to 200C/180C fan/gas 6. Put the aubergines on a baking tray and make a slit down the centre of each. Drizzle with 2 tbsp olive oil and season. Bake for 50-55 mins or until the flesh is soft. Heat the grill. Tip the tomatoes into a bowl and season well. Fill the aubergines with layers of tomatoes and mozzarella, and finish with the Parmesan. Put under the grill for 5-7 mins until the cheese is golden.

Beef in barolo

Prep:10 mins **Cook:**4 hrs and 30 mins Plus chilling

Serves 4

Ingredients

- 4 small short ribs
- 750ml bottle barolo (or another full-bodied Italian red wine)
- 1 rosemary sprig
- 1 thyme sprig
- 5 sage leaves
- 1 bay leaf
- 1 tsp black peppercorns
- 1 tsp juniper berries
- 2 tbsp vegetable oil
- 250ml chicken stock

- 2 large onions , quartered
- 2 large carrots , cut into long wedges
- soft polenta with a drizzle of truffle oil, to serve

Method

STEP 1

The night before, put the beef in a large bowl. Pour over the wine, add the herbs, peppercorns and juniper berries, and leave to soak overnight. The following day, remove the beef and pat dry, setting aside the wine and aromatics. (You can skip this step if you don't have time.)

STEP 2

Heat oven to 160C/140C fan/gas 3. Heat 1 tbsp of the vegetable oil in a large casserole. Add the beef, browning all over except for the bone side, then remove and set aside. Add the red wine, herbs, peppercorns and juniper berries. Boil for around 15 mins until reduced by half, then return the meat to the pan and add the stock. Return the mixture to the boil, then cover with a lid and cook in the oven for 2½ hrs.

STEP 3

Fry the onion and carrot in a frying pan over a high heat until golden brown, then set aside. Remove the stew from the oven and carefully lift out the meat. Sieve the remaining pan contents into a large jug, discarding the contents of the sieve. The fat from the beef will rise to the surface – skim it off. Pour the skimmed sauce back into the casserole dish, then add the browned veg and meat. Cover, then return to the oven for another 1½ hrs, removing the lid for the last 30 mins to let the sauce reduce, then serve with polenta drizzled with truffle oil.

Quick & easy tiramisu

Prep:15 mins plus 1 hr chilling, No cook

Serves 2

Ingredients

- 3 tsp instant coffee granules
- 3 tbsp coffee liqueur (or Camp Chicory & Coffee Essence)
- 250g tub mascarpone
- 85g condensed milk

- 1 tsp vanilla extract
- 4-6 sponge fingers
- 1 tbsp cocoa powder

Method

STEP 1

Mix the coffee granules with 2 tbsp boiling water in a large jug and stir to combine. Add the coffee liqueur and 75ml cold water. Pour into a shallow dish and set aside.

STEP 2

Make the cream layer by beating the mascarpone, condensed milk and vanilla extract with an electric whisk until thick and smooth.

STEP 3

Break the sponge fingers into two or three pieces and soak in the coffee mixture for a few secs. Put a few bits of the sponge in the bottom of two wine or sundae glasses and top with the cream. Sift over the cocoa and chill for at least 1 hr before serving.

Ciabatta

Prep:30 mins **Cook:**40 mins plus resting and proving

makes 2 loaves

Ingredients

For the biga

- ¼ tsp dried active yeast
- 165g plain flour
- For the dough
- ½ tsp dried action yeast
- 35ml warm milk
- 1 tbsp olive oil

- 250g strong white bread flour

Method

STEP 1

The night before, make the biga (see tip, below). Stir yeast with 50ml warm water, stand for 10 mins, then add another 80ml warm water. Gradually add the flour in a stand mixer on its lowest setting. Once it's a wet dough, transfer to a well-oiled bowl, cover and leave for 12 hours or overnight at room temperature.

STEP 2

In the morning, combine the yeast and milk and leave to stand for 10 mins. Tip into a freestanding mixer fitted with a dough hook, add 160ml water, the biga and the olive oil. Then add the flour and 1 heaped tsp salt. Use the dough hook of a stand mixer to combine the dough. Knead for 10 mins until smooth and elastic. Don't worry if it looks very wet, it should to be a very wet dough! Pour into a well-oiled bowl and cover with cling film. Leave to prove for an hour and a half or until doubled in size.

STEP 3

Once rested, begin to do a series of folds – lift the dough from the edge, pull up, over, then release it. Turn the bowl 90 degrees and do the same again. Repeat so you do a full turn of the bowl twice, or 8 folds. Rest for 30 mins, then repeat the whole folding process once more.

STEP 4

Heat the oven to 220C/200C fan/gas mark 6. Tip the dough onto a really well-floured surface and cut in half. The dough will feel like a batter and spread across the surface a bit, but don't panic, just work on a well-floured surface, using the flour and a pastry scraper to help move the dough. Shape the dough into 2 large squares (about 20cm x 20cm). Dealing with each loaf at a time, fold the dough in from each side, as if folding a booklet. Flip over, then pick up the roll and place each onto separate well-floured sheets of baking paper. The roll will be very soft, so oil or flour your hands well. Allow to rest for another 30 mins, covered with a floured tea towel. Don't worry if it spreads a little.

STEP 5

While the dough rests, heat a baking sheet in the oven. Once the dough has rested, slide each of the loaves, along with the baking paper beneath them, onto the hot baking sheet. Bake for 35-40 mins, until the crust is golden and the loaves sound hollow when tapped on the base. Move to a wire rack and cool for an hour before slicing and serving with olive oil and balsamic vinegar.

Ricotta & spinach gnudi

Prep:40 mins **Cook:**4 hrs plus 1 hr 30 mins chilling, 4 mins cooking per batch

Serves 6

Ingredients

- 500g spinach, ends trimmed
- 500g ricotta (needs to be dry, so strain overnight if it's wet)
- 75g egg yolks
- 75g dried breadcrumbs
- 50g plain flour
- whole nutmeg, for grating
- 125g Grana Padano, grated, plus extra for the sauce and to serve
- 50g butter
- 20g sage, sliced if the leaves are large

Method

STEP 1

Pour boiling water over the spinach, then leave to cool a little before squeezing out any excess liquid. Chop the spinach finely. Drain and squeeze out any excess water again. Put the spinach in a mixing bowl with the ricotta, egg yolks, breadcrumbs, flour, a grating of nutmeg, a pinch of salt and the cheese. Mix well.

STEP 2

Scoop up 24 equal-sized lumps of the mixture, using an ice cream scoop if you have one, and shape each one into a log by rolling it between your hands. Lay each log on a baking sheet, then chill for 30 mins, or until needed.

STEP 3

Bring a large pan of salted water to the boil. Lower the gnudi into the water, turn down to a simmer and cook for 3-4 mins (do this in batches if you need to). Meanwhile, heat the butter in a large frying pan, add the sage and fry until crisp. Drain the gnudi well, then tip into the pan with the sage, along with a good grating of cheese. Swirl everything together, doing it in batches if it's easier. Arrange four gnudi on each serving plate, pour over more of the sauce and scatter with more grated cheese.

Roast sea bass & vegetable traybake

Prep:10 mins **Cook:**30 mins

Serves 2

Ingredients

- 300g red-skinned potatoes, thinly sliced into rounds
- 1 red pepper, cut into strips
- 2 tbsp extra virgin olive oil
- 1 rosemary sprig, leaves removed and very finely chopped
- 2 sea bass fillets
- 25g pitted black olive, halved
- ½ lemon, sliced thinly into rounds
- handful basil leaves

Method

STEP 1

Heat oven to 180C/160C fan/gas 4. Arrange the potato and pepper slices on a large non-stick baking tray. Drizzle over 1 tbsp oil and scatter with the rosemary, a pinch of salt and a good grinding of pepper. Toss everything together well and roast for 25 mins, turning over halfway through, until the potatoes are golden and crisp at the edges.

STEP 2

Arrange the fish fillets on top and scatter over the olives. Place a couple of lemon slices on top of the fish and drizzle with the remaining oil. Roast for further 7-8 mins until the fish is cooked through. Serve scattered with basil leaves.

Italian turkey steaks with garlicky bean mash

Prep:10 mins **Cook:**10 mins

Serves 4

Ingredients

- zest 2 lemons , juice from 1 ½
- 3 tbsp olive oil
- 3 garlic cloves , crushed
- 2 tsp chopped fresh oregano , or 1 tsp dried
- 4 thick turkey steaks
- 250g punnet cherry or small plum tomatoes , some halved, some left whole
- 750g bag frozen broad bean

Method

STEP 1

Heat oven to 200C/180C fan/gas 6 and bring a pan of water to the boil. Mix most of the lemon zest with the lemon juice, oil, garlic and seasoning. Set aside two-thirds, then mix the oregano into the rest. Pour this over the turkey steaks on a plate and turn them to coat.

STEP 2

Fry the turkey steaks in a non-stick frying pan for 1-2 mins on each side to brown, then transfer to a roasting tin. Scatter the tomatoes around, then roast in the oven for 4-8 mins, depending on the thickness of the turkey, until the steaks are just cooked through.

STEP 3

Meanwhile, cook the beans in the boiling water for 4-5 mins until tender. Tip a ladle of the cooking water into a food processor, then drain the beans and tip into the processor with the reserved lemon dressing. Whizz to a mash, then divide between 4 plates and top with a turkey steak, scattering over remaining lemon zest. Shake the tin so the tomatoes roll around in the cooking juices, then serve with the turkey.

Sgroppino

Prep:5 mins **Serves 1**

Ingredients

- 2 tsp lemon sorbet

- 1 tsp vodka
- champagne

Method

STEP 1

Put the lemon sorbet into the bottom of a champagne flute.

STEP 2

Pour over the vodka, then top with champagne.

Classic spaghetti Bolognese

Prep:10 mins **Cook:**1 hr

Serves 4

Ingredients

- 2 tbsp oil
- 1 large onion, finely chopped
- 2 celery sticks, finely chopped
- 2 carrots, finely chopped
- 50g pancetta cubes
- 400g lean beef mince
- 150g chicken livers, chopped, fat and sinew removed
- 1 large bay leaves
- 4 tbsp tomato purée
- 150ml white wine
- 500ml fresh chicken stock
- 300ml passata
- 500g pack spaghetti
- 50ml full-fat milk
- parmesan, grated, to serve

Method

STEP 1

Heat 1½ tbsp oil in a large pan or flameproof casserole dish over a low-medium heat. Add the onion, celery and carrots with a pinch of salt. Cook for 10 mins, stirring occasionally, until softened but not coloured. Transfer to a plate using a slotted spoon.

STEP 2

Pour the remaining oil into the pan, increase the heat and tip in the pancetta. Cook for 3-4 mins until golden. Add the mince and chicken livers, and cook for a further 5 mins until browned, breaking down the mince with the back of a wooden spoon.

STEP 3

Return the vegetables to the pan and add the bay leaf and tomato purée. Cook for a 1 min more and mix well. Pour in the wine and reduce by half. Add the stock and passata with some seasoning and bring to the boil. Reduce the heat to medium and let the sauce bubble away for 35-40 mins, stirring occasionally, until reduced by half and you are left with a thick ragu.

STEP 4

Bring a large saucepan of salted water to the boil 15 mins before the sauce is ready. Drop in the pasta, cook following pack instructions until al dente, then drain.

STEP 5

To finish the sauce, stir in the milk and season to taste. Tip the pasta onto a plate and top with the Bolognese. Serve with the Parmesan.

Best ever tiramisu

Prep:30 mins Plus chilling **Serves 6**

Ingredients

- 568ml pot double cream
- 250g tub mascarpone
- 75ml marsala
- 5 tbsp golden caster sugar
- 300ml strong coffee, made with 2 tbsp coffee granules and 300ml boiling water
- 175g pack sponge fingers
- 25g dark chocolate
- 2 tsp cocoa powder

Method

STEP 1

Put the double cream, mascarpone, marsala and golden caster sugar in a large bowl.

STEP 2

Whisk until the cream and mascarpone have completely combined and have the consistency of thickly whipped cream.

STEP 3

Pour the coffee into a shallow dish. Dip in a few of the sponge fingers at a time, turning for a few seconds until they are nicely soaked, but not soggy. Layer these in a dish until you've used half the sponge fingers, then spread over half of the creamy mixture.

STEP 4

Using the coarse side of the grater, grate over most of the dark chocolate. Then repeat the layers (you should use up all the coffee), finishing with the creamy layer.

STEP 5

Cover and chill for a few hours or overnight. Will keep in the fridge for up to two days.

STEP 6

To serve, dust with the cocoa powder and grate over the remainder of the chocolate.

Italian turkey toasties

Prep:10 mins **Cook:**10 mins

Ingredients

- 4 slices prosciutto
- 4 turkey breast steaks
- 4 tbsp pepperonata antipasto (such as Scala)
- 125g ball reduced-fat mozzarella , sliced into 8
- small bunch basil , leaves only
- medium ciabatta loaf, or 2 ciabatta rolls

- salad leaves , to serve

Method

STEP 1

Heat grill to high. Lay the prosciutto out on a large baking sheet and sit a turkey steak on top, crossways. Spread the turkey with the pepperonata, then top with 2 slices of mozzarella, a few basil leaves and some seasoning. Fold the ends of the prosciutto around the cheese to enclose. Grill for 10 mins until golden and cooked through. Leave to rest for 2 mins.

STEP 2

Cut the ciabatta into 4 or the rolls in half, then toast under the grill. Top with salad leaves, then sit the turkey on top and serve.

Pesto chicken stew with cheesy dumplings

Prep:50 mins **Cook:**2 hrs and 20 mins

Serves 8

Ingredients

- 2 tbsp olive oil
- 12-15 chicken thighs , skin removed, bone in
- 200g smoked bacon lardon or chopped bacon
- 1 large onion , chopped
- 4 celery sticks, chopped
- 3 leeks , chopped
- 4 tbsp plain flour
- 200ml white wine
- 1l chicken stock
- 2 bay leaves
- 200g frozen pea
- 140g sundried tomato
- 140g fresh pesto
- small bunch basil , chopped

For the dumplings

- 140g butter
- 250g self-raising flour
- 100g parmesan , grated
- 50g pine nut

Method

STEP 1

Heat the oil in a large casserole dish. Brown the chicken until golden on all sides – you might have to do this in batches – remove the chicken from the pan as you go and set aside.

STEP 2

Add the lardons to the pan and sizzle for a few mins, then add the onion, celery and leeks, and cook over a medium heat for 8-10 mins until the vegetables have softened. Stir in the flour, season and cook for a further 2 mins.

STEP 3

Gradually stir in the wine and allow it to bubble away, then stir in the stock. Return the chicken to the pan with the bay leaves and cover with a lid. Reduce the heat and simmer gently for 1½ hrs or until the chicken is tender. The stew can now be cooled and frozen if you're making ahead. Just defrost thoroughly, then gently warm through back in the pan before continuing.

STEP 4

Heat oven to 200C/180C fan/gas 6. Add the peas, sundried tomatoes, pesto and basil to the stew. To make the dumplings, rub the butter into the flour until it resembles fine breadcrumbs. Mix in the grated cheese and add 150ml water, mixing with a cutlery knife to bring the crumbs together to form a light and sticky dough. Break off walnut-sized lumps and shape into small balls. Roll the tops of the dumplings in the pine nuts so a few stick to the outside, then place the dumplings on top of the stew and scatter with any remaining nuts. Put the dish in the oven and bake for 25 mins until the dumplings are golden brown and cooked through. Serve with mashed potato and extra veg if you like.

Low-fat turkey bolognese

Prep:10 mins **Cook:**45 mins

Serves 4 - 6

Ingredients

- 400g lean turkey mince (choose breast instead of thigh mince if you can, as it has less fat)
- 2 tsp vegetable oil
- 1 large onion, chopped
- 1 large carrot, chopped
- 3 celery sticks, chopped
- 250g pack brown mushroom, finely chopped
- pinch of sugar
- 1 tbsp tomato purée
- 2 x 400g cans chopped tomato with garlic & herbs
- 400ml chicken stock, made from 1 low-sodium stock cube
- cooked wholemeal pasta and fresh basil leaves (optional), to serve

Method

STEP 1

Heat a large non-stick frying pan and dry-fry the turkey mince until browned. Tip onto a plate and set aside.

STEP 2

Add the oil and gently cook the onion, carrot and celery until softened, about 10 mins (add a splash of water if it starts to stick). Add the mushrooms and cook for a few mins, then add the sugar and tomato purée, and cook for 1 min more, stirring to stop it from sticking.

STEP 3

Add the tomatoes, turkey and stock with some seasoning. Simmer for at least 20 mins (or longer) until thickened. Serve with the pasta and fresh basil, if you have it.

Focaccia with pesto & mozzarella

Prep:20 mins - 25 mins **Cook:**30 mins Plus rising and proving

Serves 4 - 6

Ingredients

- 500g strong white bread flour, plus some for dusting

- 1 ½ tsp salt
- 7g sachet fast-action yeast
- 2 tbsp extra-virgin olive oil , plus some for drizzling
- 125g ball mozzarella , drained
- 5 tbsp pesto (shop-bought or see recipe, below)
- sea salt , to serve (optional)

Method

STEP 1

Put the flour into a bowl and mix in the salt. Mix the yeast into 325ml tepid water. Add the water and oil to the flour, then mix well with a plastic scraper or your hands. When most of the liquid is incorporated, use your hands to bring all the ingredients together into a ball of dough.

STEP 2

Tip the dough out onto a worktop lightly dusted with flour and work it by pulling and stretching for at least 10 mins. Try to get as much air into it as possible. Put the ball of worked dough into a well-oiled bowl, cover with a little more oil and a tea towel or cling film. Leave to rest for 1 hr or so in a non-draughty warm spot, until doubled in size.

STEP 3

Now stretch the dough out onto a baking sheet until it's about 20 x 30cm. Leave the dough to rise again to about half as high again, about 30-40 mins in a warm draught-free place, loosely covered with a tea towel.

STEP 4

Heat oven to 180C/160C fan/gas 4. When the dough has risen, press your fingers into it gently to make some holes. Bake for about 15 mins, then remove from the oven. Tear over the mozzarella, then bake for another 5-10 mins until golden and cooked through. Drizzle over the pesto and scatter with sea salt, if you like. Serve straight away.

Sherry, almond & orange pandoro

Prep:10 mins **Cook:**5 mins

Serves 12 - 15

Ingredients

- 300ml double cream
- 250g mascarpone
- 4 tbsp Pedro Ximénez sherry
- 1 large orange , zested
- 2 tbsp icing sugar , plus extra for dusting
- 1 pandoro
- 50g almonds , toasted and roughly chopped
- edible gold leaf (optional)

Method

STEP 1

In a large bowl, whisk together the cream, mascarpone, half the sherry, 3/ 4 of the zest and the icing sugar until the mixture is floppy and just holds its shape.

STEP 2

Cut the pandoro horizontally into five slices. Put the bottom piece on a serving plate or cake stand and drizzle over a little of the remaining sherry. Spoon over a quarter of the cream mixture and top with a handful of the almonds (saving enough for each layer and to decorate the top). Add the next layer of pandoro and continue to sandwich the layers together, rotating each at a different angle so that you create the shape of a Christmas tree.

STEP 3

Dust with icing sugar, then dot over the gold leaf (if using) along with the remaining almonds and orange zest.

Squash, pea & feta frittatinis

Prep:20 mins **Cook:**25 mins plus cooling

Makes 8

Ingredients

- 250g butternut squash , peeled, deseeded and chopped into small pieces
- 25g frozen peas

- 100g feta , crumbled
- 4 large eggs

Method

STEP 1

Heat oven to 200C/180C fan/gas 6. Put the butternut squash in a bowl, cover with cling film and cook in the microwave on High for 5-7 mins until tender. Meanwhile, line 8 holes of a muffin tin with squares of baking parchment – allow a little overhang at the top as the frittatinis will puff up.

STEP 2

Divide the squash, peas and feta between the lined muffin holes – they should be quite full. Beat the eggs in a jug with some seasoning, then pour into the muffin holes. Put the tin in the centre of the oven and bake for 20 mins. Leave to cool for about 15 mins before packing into a cooler bag for transporting, or chill for up to 24 hrs.

Walnut & red pepper pesto pasta

Prep:15 mins **Cook:**15 mins

Serves 4

Ingredients

- 400g strozzapreti or casarecce pasta , or another short pasta shape
- 100g walnut
- 3 roasted red peppers , roughly chopped
- 25g parmesan , or a vegetarian alternative, plus extra to serve
- 1 small garlic clove , roughly chopped
- large pack basil , plus a few leaves to serve
- 2 tbsp extra virgin olive oil
- 50g mascarpone

Method

STEP 1

Cook the pasta following pack instructions. Meanwhile, toast the walnuts in a dry pan for a few mins. Add half the walnuts to the small bowl of a food processor or a hand chopper, along with the red peppers, Parmesan, garlic, basil, oil and some seasoning. Whizz to a paste, adding a splash of water from the pasta if it is a little dry.

STEP 2

Drain the pasta, reserving a cup of the cooking water. Return the pasta to the pan and set over a low heat. Add the pesto, mascarpone and 3-4 tbsp of the reserved pasta water, then stir until the mascarpone has melted, adding a splash more pasta water if the sauce needs thinning. To serve, crush the remaining walnuts in your hand and scatter over the pasta with a few more basil leaves and some extra Parmesan.

Cannoli

Prep:40 mins **Cook:**30 mins plus resting and cooling

Makes 12

Ingredients

- 150g plain flour
- 1 tbsp golden caster sugar
- large pinch bicarbonate of soda
- ½ tsp cinnamon
- 1 tsp cocoa powder (optional)
- 30g butter
- 1 egg, separated
- 50ml dry marsala or white wine
- rapeseed oil or sunflower oil for deep-frying (see tip)
- 50g dark chocolate, melted
- handful pistachio kernels, finely chopped
- icing sugar, to dust

For the filling

- 250g ricotta, drained and beaten until fluffy
- 100g mascarpone
- 2 tbsp finely chopped candied peel

- 2 tbsp icing sugar

You will also need

- cannoli moulds (available to buy online)

Method

STEP 1

Tip the flour, sugar, bicarb, cinnamon and cocoa (if using) into a bowl with a pinch of salt. Add the butter and rub it into the dry ingredients until there are no more lumps. Mix the egg yolk and marsala and add this to the bowl, then mix the whole lot together and knead to a smooth dough. Wrap and rest in the fridge. (Can be made ahead and fried the next day.)

STEP 2

Fill a deep-fat fryer, wok or deep saucepan a third of the way up with oil. Cut the dough into pieces and, working one piece at a time, roll them out as thinly as you can – use a pasta machine if you have one. Heat the oil and keep an eye on it until it reaches 180C. Lay the dough out on a lightly floured surface and cut out circles about 11cm across. Wrap each one around a cannoli mould, using some of the egg white to stick the top edge down and they're ready for frying.

It's important to take care when cooking with hot oil. Read our guide on how to deep-fry safely to avoid accidents in the kitchen.

STEP 3

Deep-fry the cannoli (with their moulds) one at a time, making sure they cook all over. They should take about 45-60 seconds in all and should be visibly golden brown (keep cooking a little longer if they aren't) and the dough will bubble and blister. Carefully take each one out of the oil using the tongs and shake the cannoli off the mould very carefully onto kitchen paper. As you fry each one, make sure the oil stays at 180C at all times and doesn't get any hotter. These will keep for 2-3 days in an airtight container.

STEP 4

When the cannoli are cold, dip the end of each one into chocolate, then dip some of those into the pistachios. Leave to cool and harden. Beat the ricotta and mascarpone together, then stir in the candied peel and sugar. Spoon the mixture into a piping bag with a wide star nozzle and pipe it into the cannoli. Serve soon after filling.

Pumpkin, fennel & Taleggio galette

Prep:35 mins **Cook:**1 hr and 30 mins

Serves 6

Ingredients

- 700g pumpkin or 1 small squash
- 5 tbsp olive oil
- grating of nutmeg
- 2 small fennel bulbs
- juice ½ small lemon
- ½ tsp fennel seeds , toasted and coarsely crushed
- 470g spinach , coarse stalks removed
- 15g unsalted butter
- 1 garlic clove , crushed
- 1 egg yolk mixed with 2 tsp milk (to make an egg wash)
- 200g Taleggio (or vegetarian alternative), sliced
- 375g puff pastry

Method

STEP 1

Heat oven to 190C/170C fan/gas 5. Peel the squash, then halve and deseed it before cutting the flesh into thick wedges and halving them again to make quarters. Put the slices in a roasting tin with half the olive oil, the nutmeg and seasoning, and toss to coat. Roast for 30 mins, or until tender and a little caramelised.

STEP 2

Halve the fennel bulbs lengthways and remove the tops and tough outer leaves from each piece. Trim the base and cut each half into thick wedges, keeping them intact at the base. Put the wedges straight into a bowl and toss with the lemon juice to prevent discolouring. Add the fennel seeds, remaining olive oil and some seasoning, then toss well. Spread the fennel in a roasting tin large enough to hold it in a single layer and cover with foil. Roast the fennel (at the same time as the squash) for 20 mins, or until tender with pale -gold undersides.

STEP 3

Wash the spinach and cook in a covered pan over a medium heat for 1-2 mins. When wilted, drain in a colander and leave to cool. Squeeze the excess moisture out of the spinach, chop roughly and season. Melt the butter in a frying pan and quickly fry the spinach with the garlic for 3 mins. Set aside.

STEP 4

Roll out the pastry to make the base of the tart, ending up with a piece measuring roughly 28 x 38cm. Put the pastry base on to a floured metal baking sheet. Create a border all the way round by lightly running a knife 2cm from the edge. Prick the rest of the pastry all over with a fork. Put a rectangle of baking parchment, the size of the inside of the border, over the pastry. Weight it down with baking beans. Knock up the sides of the pastry by holding a small knife at a right angle to the pastry and making small indentations to release the layers. This will give you a better rise. Paint the border with the egg wash.

STEP 5

Put the pastry in the preheated oven and cook for 25 mins, removing the beans and paper after 15 mins. Take the partially cooked tart base out of the oven and, if the centre has risen, gently flatten it with the back of a wooden spoon. Turn the oven up to 200C/180C fan/gas 6.

STEP 6

Spoon the spinach onto the pastry, then put the squash and fennel on top. Distribute the cheese over the top, too. Put the tart back into the oven and cook for a further 25 mins. The cheese should be golden in patches and the pastry should be cooked and golden, but not too dark.

Prosecco cake

Prep:30 mins **Cook:**45 mins - 50 mins

Serves 18

Ingredients

- 350g unsalted butter , plus a little for the tins
- 350g golden caster sugar
- 6 eggs
- 350g self-raising flour
- 100ml prosecco
- 100g raspberry jam

For the buttercream

- 300g unsalted butter , softened
- 600g icing sugar
- 100ml prosecco
- To decorate
- sprinkles , coloured sugar, mini meringues, Prosecco-flavoured sweets, popcorn and lollies

Method

STEP 1

Heat oven to 160C/140C fan/gas 3. Butter the inside of 2 deep, loose bottomed 21cm tins. Cream the butter and sugar together with electric beaters until it is light and fluffy, then gradually beat in the eggs a little at a time. Fold in the flour and a pinch of salt, don't worry if the mixture look like it has split, it will come back together when the flour is added. Pour in the Prosecco and stir until smooth.

STEP 2

Spoon the mixture into the tins, level the top and bake for 45-50 mins or until the cakes are well-risen and golden and a skewer inserted comes out clean. Leave to cool in the tin for 10 minutes and then turn them out onto a rack.

STEP 3

While the cakes cool, make the icing. Beat the butter with the icing sugar until it is smooth. Add the Prosecco and beat again until the frosting is fluffy and smooth.

STEP 4

Level the cakes if you need to and spread the raspberry jam on one of the cakes followed by some of the butter cream, sandwich the other cake on top. Roughly ice the cake all over in a very thin layer with a couple of tablespoons of buttercream, this will help all the crumbs stick to the cake and help make the outer layer of icing nice and clean. Ice the cake all over with the remaining buttercream, this can be quite rough because you are going to stick sweet all over it. Now stick sweets all over it. Go mad. Drink Prosecco with it.

Strawberry panna cotta

Prep:30 mins **Cook:**25 mins plus cooling and 3 hrs chilling

Serves 6

Ingredients

For the panna cotta

- 3 gelatine leaves
- 450ml double cream
- 200ml whole milk
- 100g white caster sugar
- 1 vanilla pod

For the strawberries

- 400g strawberry , hulled and halved, or quartered if very large
- 1 ½ tsp cornflour
- 50g white caster sugar

Method

STEP 1

For the panna cotta, put the gelatine leaves in a small bowl of cold water to soften – this will take about 5 mins. Meanwhile, pour the cream, milk and sugar into a pan, split the vanilla pod, scrape out the seeds and add, along with the pod, to the cream mixture. Heat gently until hot, but not bubbling. Remove the gelatine leaves from the water, squeeze out any excess liquid then add, one at a time, to the hot cream. Stir until dissolved. Leave to stand for 20-30 mins until cooled – the vanilla pods should be suspended in the liquid by this point. Strain the mixture through a sieve into 6 serving glasses, then chill for at least 3 hrs.

STEP 2

Toss the strawberries with the cornflour and sugar in a saucepan. Place over a medium heat and cook for 4-5 mins, until the released juices thicken and the strawberries soften. Set aside to cool. Once completely cooled, top the set panna cottas with the strawberry mixture. Chill until ready to serve.

Beefy melanzane parmigiana

Prep:20 mins **Cook:**1 hr and 50 mins

Serves 6

Ingredients

- 2 tbsp olive oil , plus extra for brushing
- 800g beef mince
- 3 garlic cloves , crushed
- 3 thyme sprigs
- 3 rosemary sprigs
- 3 bay leaves
- 2 x 400g cans chopped tomato
- glass of red wine
- 1 beef stock cube
- 1 tbsp sugar
- 5 aubergines , sliced lengthways into 5mm slices
- 2 x 125g balls mozzarella , torn into small chunks
- 50g parmesan , grated
- 250g tub mascarpone

Method

STEP 1

Heat the oil in a large frying pan or flameproof casserole dish. Add the mince and brown over a high heat, breaking up with a wooden spoon as you go. (You may need to do this in batches.) Once well browned, tip onto a plate.

STEP 2

Add the remaining oil, the garlic and herbs to the pan and gently cook for 1 min. Tip in the tomatoes and red wine, and bring to a simmer, stirring up any meaty bits stuck to the bottom of the pan. Return the mince to the pan, crumble in the stock cube, and add sugar and seasoning. Gently simmer for at least 1 hr, stirring occasionally, splashing in more water to keep it saucy if you need to. If you have time to simmer for longer, go for it – the longer the better. Fish out the herb stalks and bay leaves.

STEP 3

Meanwhile, heat a griddle or frying pan. Brush the aubergine slices on both sides with olive oil, then griddle in batches. You want each slice softened and slightly charred, so don't have the heat too high or the aubergine will char before softening. Remove to a plate as you go.

STEP 4

Heat oven to 180C/160C fan/gas 4. Set aside some of each cheese to go on the top. In a large baking dish spread a spoonful of mince sauce over the base then top with a layer of aubergines and season well. Spoon over some more mince sauce, then scatter over some mozzarella, Parmesan and blobs of mascarpone. Add another layer of aubergines and some seasoning. Repeat, layering everything up and finish with a layer of meat sauce. Top with your reserved cheese and bake for 30-40 mins until the top is crisp and golden and mince bubbling.

Seared steak with celery & pepper caponata

Prep:10 mins **Cook:**30 mins

Serves 2

Ingredients

- 200g extra-lean fillet steak
- 140g fresh spinach
- For the caponata
- 1-cal oil spray
- 1 red onion , halved and sliced
- 2 garlic cloves , cut into slivers
- 400g can chopped tomato
- 2 celery sticks, sliced
- 1 orange pepper , deseeded, quartered and sliced
- 25g pitted black kalamata olive , halved (about 8)
- 1 tbsp caper
- ½ tsp dried oregano or 1 tbsp fresh
- 1 tsp balsamic vinegar

Method

STEP 1

For the caponata, spray a large, wide non-stick pan with 3 sprays of oil, and add the onion and garlic. Cover and cook for 5 mins, stirring halfway through to brown them.

STEP 2

Tip in the tomatoes and a can of water, then stir in all the other caponata ingredients. Cover the pan and leave to simmer for 30 mins.

STEP 3

Heat a griddle or small non-stick frying pan. Generously grind black pepper over the steak and sear on both sides, about 6 mins in total, until cooked to your liking. Allow to rest while you wilt the spinach in a covered pan on a low heat.

STEP 4

Spoon the caponata onto 2 serving plates, top with the spinach, then slice the beef and arrange on top.

Sausage sandwich with pesto

Prep:5 mins **Cook:**10 mins

Serves 1

Ingredients

- 2 herby Cumberland sausages , sliced in half lengthways
- 1 ciabatta roll , sliced in half
- 2 tbsp fresh pesto
- 1 roasted red pepper from a jar, sliced in half
- ½ x 125g ball mozzarella , sliced
- handful rocket

Method

STEP 1

Heat grill to high. Put the sausages on a baking sheet, cut-side down, and grill for 5-6 mins or until cooked through, then set aside. Lay the ciabatta roll halves, cut-side up, on a baking tray and spread each with pesto. Top each half with a pepper and mozzarella slice, then grill for 2 mins or until golden and bubbling. Add the sausages and a handful of rocket, and put the roll back together, pressing down firmly to hold the fillings in place.

Aubergine rolls with spinach & ricotta

Prep:15 mins **Cook:**45 mins

Serves 4

Ingredients

- 2 aubergines , cut into thin slices lengthways
- 2 tbsp olive oil
- 500g spinach
- 250g tub ricotta
- grating of nutmeg
- 350g jar tomato sauce
- 4 tbsp fresh breadcrumb
- 4 tbsp parmesan (or vegetarian alternative)

Method

STEP 1

Heat oven to 220C/200C fan/gas 7. Brush both sides of the aubergine slices with oil, then lay on a large baking sheet. Bake for 15-20 mins until tender, turning once.

STEP 2

Meanwhile, put the spinach in a large colander and pour over a kettle of boiling water to wilt. Cool, then squeeze out the excess water, so that it is dry. Mix with the ricotta, nutmeg and plenty of seasoning.

STEP 3

Dollop a spoonful of the cheesy spinach mix in the centre of each aubergine slice, fold over to make a parcel and lay, sealed-side down, in an ovenproof dish. Pour over tomato sauce, sprinkle with breadcrumbs and cheese, and bake for 20-25 mins until golden and piping hot.

Mushroom, ricotta & rocket tart

Prep:10 mins **Cook:**25 mins

Serves 4

Ingredients

- 1 sheet ready-rolled puff pastry
- 2 tbsp olive oil
- 525g family pack mushroom , halved or quartered if large
- 2 garlic cloves , 1 finely sliced, 1 crushed
- 250g tub ricotta
- good grating of nutmeg
- ¼ small pack parsley , leaves only, roughly chopped
- 50g rocket

Method

STEP 1

Heat oven to 220C/200C fan/gas 7 and place a baking sheet inside. Unroll the pastry onto a piece of baking parchment and score a border around the pastry about 1.5cm in from the edge. Place the pastry (still on the parchment) on the baking sheet and cook for 10-15 mins.

STEP 2

While the pastry bakes, heat the oil in a large lidded pan and cook the mushrooms for 2-3 mins, with the lid on, stirring occasionally. Remove the lid and add the sliced garlic, then cook for 1 min more to get rid of excess liquid.

STEP 3

Mix the crushed garlic with the ricotta and nutmeg, then season well. Remove the pastry from the oven and carefully push down the risen centre. Spread over the ricotta mixture, then spoon on the mushrooms and garlic. Bake for 5 mins, then scatter over the parsley and rocket.

Raspberry & lemon polenta cake

Prep:15 mins **Cook:**30 mins

Serves 8

Ingredients

For the cake

- 225g very soft butter
- 225g caster sugar , plus 1 tbsp
- 4 eggs , beaten
- 175g fine polenta
- 50g plain flour
- 1½ tsp baking powder
- ½ tsp vanilla extract
- finely grated zest of 1½ lemons
- 200g frozen raspberry , left frozen
- icing sugar , or more to taste (optional)

For the filling

- 100g soft cheese at room temperature (we used Philadelphia)
- 1 tbsp icing sugar , or more to taste
- finely grated zest of ½ lemon , plus a squeeze of juice
- 142ml tub double cream
- 100g frozen raspberry , defrosted

Method

STEP 1

Heat oven to 190C/fan 170C/gas 5 and butter two 20cm sandwich tins. Line the bottom of the tins with baking paper. In a large bowl, beat the butter and 225g caster sugar together until creamy and light. Gradually add the egg, little by little, until all the egg is worked in and the mix is pale and fluffy. If the mix looks like it's starting to split, add 1 tsp of the flour, then carry on.

STEP 2

Put the polenta in another bowl, then stir in the flour and baking powder. Beat the vanilla extract and zest into the eggy mix, then fold in the dry ingredients. Spoon half the batter into each tin and level the top. Scatter all but a handful of the raspberries over the mix and poke in gently. Sprinkle one of the sponges with the 1 tbsp sugar. Bake for 20 mins until risen and golden, but still with a little wobble under the crust.

STEP 3

Open the oven, whip out the sugar-crusted sponge and quickly poke the remaining frozen raspberries into the top. Bake both sponges for 10 more mins or until springy in the middle. If this sounds too tricky, just leave the sponges to bake for 30 mins – the cake won't look as glam, but will still taste great (you can add the leftover berries to the filling instead). Cool in the tin for 10 mins, then cool completely on a rack. Be careful when turning out the raspberry-topped sponge and slide it off its base rather than turning it upside down.

STEP 4

When the sponges are cold, beat the soft cheese with the icing sugar, lemon zest and a little of the juice to loosen if it needs it. Very lightly whip the cream so that it just holds its shape, then fold into the cheese. Fold in the defrosted raspberries. Use to sandwich the sponges together, sugar-crusted on top, and serve dusted with more icing sugar.

Pizza dough

Prep: 15 mins plus rising (no cook)

Makes 4 pizzas

Ingredients

- 500g '00' flour or plain flour, plus extra for dusting
- 1 tsp salt
- ½ tsp dried yeast (not fast-action)
- 400ml warm water
- oil, for greasing

Method

STEP 1

It's easiest to make this in a standing mixer with a dough hook (otherwise mix it in a bowl and knead on your work surface). Put the flour and salt in the bowl and mix the yeast into the water. It's always a good idea to wait 5 mins before using the liquid to see if the yeast is working – little bits will start to rise to the top and you'll know it's active.

STEP 2

Turn on the motor and pour in the liquid. Keep the speed on medium-high and it should come together as a ball. If the bottom is still sticking, tip in 1-2 tbsp of flour. Knead for 5-7 mins until the dough is shiny and it springs back when you press your finger into it. (If kneading by hand, it will take you about 10 mins.) Try not to add too much flour if you can. This is a slightly sticky dough, but that keeps it light and it rises beautifully.

STEP 3

Use oiled hands to remove the dough from the hook and bowl. Oil another bowl and place the dough in it. Turn it around so that it's lightly coated in the oil. Cover tightly with cling film and then a tea towel. Place in a draught-free area that's warm and leave until the dough has doubled in size. If it's a hot day, it should only take 2 hrs to rise, but it could take 4 hrs if it's cold. (If you don't plan to use the dough for a day or two, place it in the fridge straight away; take it out 3-4 hrs before using. Punch it down first and bring it together on a floured surface.)

STEP 4

Divide the dough into 2 pieces for big pizzas or 4 for plate-sized ones, then shape into balls (see Shaping the dough in tips, below) – dust them in flour as they will be sticky. Keep them covered with a tea towel or cling film while you prepare the toppings. (you can also freeze them in sealed bags. Just thaw in the fridge on the day, then bring to room temperature 3 hrs before using.)

STEP 5

To shape the dough: If you want to get air pockets and a light but crisp dough, then don't use a rolling pin. It flattens and pops the air bubbles. (Two days in the fridge will produce the most air bubbles – take it out three to four hours before using.) If your dough is at room temperature, you can use your fingers to gently stretch the dough out. Once it's about 16cm, place the disc over the tops of your hands (not palm side) and use them to stretch it further, up to about 25cm. You can start pressing out the other discs, then wait to do the final bit when you're ready to cook. Once you've mastered stretching the dough out, you can experiment with other shapes: rectangles, rounds or squares all look authentic.

STEP 6

To cook the pizza: An outdoor gas barbecue is best for controlling the temperature, but charcoal will give your pizza a more authentic, smoky flavour. For gas, turn the flames down to medium-low so that the bottom of the pizza doesn't burn. When cooking on a charcoal barbecue, let the coals turn grey before you pop on the pizza.

STEP 7

Place the pizza on a floured baking sheet (with no edge) or a pizza peel – this is a flat pizza paddle with a long handle, which makes it easier to get the dough on and off the grill. The flour will provide the 'wheels' for it to slide onto the grill – don't use oil as it sticks more and won't transfer as well.

STEP 8

Make sure the grill is hot and the flames have died back if cooking on charcoal. Slide the dough onto the grill, close the lid (if your barbecue has one) and give it three to four minutes. The dough will puff up; it's ready when the bottom has light brown stripes. Use tongs to pull the dough off and turn it upside down.

STEP 9

Assemble the pizza of your choice – see 'Goes well with', right, for topping suggestions. Remember that less is more, as the dough will stay crisper and the toppings will cook better.

STEP 10

Place the pizza back on the grill, uncooked-side down, and shut the lid. Give it another three to four minutes, then remove when the cheese is melted and the toppings are hot.

Roasted tomato, basil & Parmesan quiche

Prep:40 mins **Cook:**40 mins

Serves 8

Ingredients

- 300g cherry tomato
- drizzle olive oil
- 50g parmesan (or vegetarian alternative), grated
- 2 eggs
- 284ml pot double cream
- handful basil leaves, shredded, plus a few small ones left whole for scattering

For the pastry

- 280g plain flour, plus extra for dusting
- 140g cold butter, cut into pieces

Method

STEP 1

To make the pastry, tip the flour and butter into a bowl, then rub together with your fingertips until completely mixed and crumbly. Add 8 tbsp cold water, then bring everything together with your hands until just combined. Roll into a ball and use straight away or chill for up to 2 days. The pastry can also be frozen for up to a month.

STEP 2

Roll out the pastry on a lightly floured surface to a round about 5cm larger than a 25cm tin. Use your rolling pin to lift it up, then drape over the tart case so there is an overhang of pastry on the sides. Using a small ball of pastry scraps, push the pastry into the corners of the tin. Chill in the fridge or freezer for 20 mins. Heat oven to 200C/fan 180C/gas 6.

STEP 3

In a small roasting tin, drizzle the tomatoes with olive oil and season with salt and pepper. Put the tomatoes in a low shelf of the oven.

STEP 4

Lightly prick the base of the tart with a fork, line the tart case with a large circle of greaseproof paper or foil, then fill with baking beans. Blind-bake the tart for 20 mins, remove the paper and beans, then continue to cook for 5-10 mins until biscuit brown.

STEP 5

When you remove the tart case from the oven, take out the tomatoes, too.

STEP 6

While the tart is cooking, beat the eggs in a large bowl. Gradually add the cream, then stir in the basil and season. When the case is ready, sprinkle half the cheese over the base, scatter over the tomatoes, pour over the cream mix, then finally scatter over the rest of the cheese. Bake for 20-25 mins until set and golden brown. Leave to cool in the case, trim the edges of the pastry, then remove from the tin. Scatter over the remaining basil and serve in slices.

Rosemary chicken with tomato sauce

Prep:5 mins **Cook:**30 mins

Serves 4

Ingredients

- 1 tbsp olive oil
- 8 boneless, skinless chicken thighs
- 1 rosemary sprig, leaves finely chopped
- 1 red onion, finely sliced
- 3 garlic cloves, sliced
- 2 anchovy fillets, chopped
- 400g can chopped tomatoes
- 1 tbsp capers, drained
- 75ml red wine (optional)

Method

STEP 1

Heat half the oil in a non-stick pan, then brown the chicken all over. Add half the chopped rosemary, stir to coat, then set aside on a plate.

STEP 2

In the same pan, heat the rest of the oil, then gently cook the onion for about 5 mins until soft. Add the garlic, anchovies and remaining rosemary, then fry for a few mins more until fragrant. Pour in the tomatoes and capers with the wine, if using, or 75ml water if not. Bring to the boil, then return the chicken pieces to the pan. Cover, then cook for 20 mins until the chicken is cooked through. Season and serve with a crisp green salad and crusty bread.

Penne with chorizo & broccoli

Prep:5 mins **Cook:**20 mins

Serves 4

Ingredients

- 400g penne
- small head of broccoli , broken into small florets
- 200g cooking chorizo , diced
- 2 garlic cloves , crushed

- 1 tbsp fennel seed
- 200g low-fat cream cheese with garlic & herbs
- parmesan and rocket leaves, to serve

Method

STEP 1

Cook the penne following pack instructions, adding the broccoli for the final 3 mins. When cooked, drain, reserving a splash of the cooking water.

STEP 2

Meanwhile, fry the chorizo in a large dry frying pan until it starts to turn golden and release its oils. Add the garlic and fennel seeds, and cook for 1 min more. When the penne is cooked, tip it into the pan with the chorizo. Add the cream cheese, stir together until melted, adding a splash of the reserved cooking water so the sauce coats the pasta.

STEP 3

Serve in bowls, scattered with a few rocket leaves and some grated Parmesan, if you like.

Rye pizza with figs, fennel, gorgonzola & hazelnuts

Prep:1 hr **Cook:**45 mins plus 2-3 hrs rising

makes 2 x 30cm pizzas

Ingredients

For the dough

- 5g active dried yeast
- 250g strong white flour
- 125g '00' flour
- 125g rye flour
- ½ tsp sugar
- 1 tsp olive oil
- semolina flour , for dusting

For the topping

- 1 large fennel bulb , any fronds reserved
- juice 1/2 small lemon
- 1 tbsp olive oil
- 2 medium onions , halved and very finely sliced
- ¼ tsp fennel seeds , coarsely crushed in a mortar
- a little extra virgin olive oil , for drizzling
- 12 small figs , halved
- 1 ½ tbsp balsamic vinegar
- a little caster sugar , for sprinkling
- 180g gorgonzola (or vegetarian alternative), broken into chunks
- 2 tbsp hazelnuts , halved and toasted

Method

STEP 1

To make the dough, mix the yeast in a small bowl with 2 tbsp warm water and 1 tbsp strong white flour. Leave somewhere warm to 'sponge' for 20 mins or so (this dissolves and activates the yeast). Tip the three flours into a large bowl and make a well in the centre. Pour in the sponged yeast, 1 tsp salt, sugar, oil and 290ml warm water, and mix to form a wet dough. Knead for 10 mins until satiny and elastic, then put in a clean bowl, cover with a cloth and leave to double in size for 2 1/2 - 3 hrs.

STEP 2

Quarter the fennel bulb lengthways and remove any tough outer leaves. Trim the base of each, thinly slice with a knife or mandolin, then put in a bowl with the lemon juice so it doesn't turn brown.

STEP 3

Heat the oil in a frying pan, add the onions and a pinch of salt, and fry over a medium heat for 7 mins. Add 1-2 tbsp of water, season with pepper, cover and cook on a low heat for 10 mins until softened. Add most of the fennel, along with the fennel seeds and seasoning, and cook for 3 mins, stirring every so often. If the mixture is still wet, uncover and bubble off any liquid.

STEP 4

An hour before cooking, heat the oven to its highest setting and put a baking sheet or pizza stone in to heat. Tip the dough onto a lightly floured surface, knead it a little, then halve and roll each piece into a circle or rough square. Lift the dough and, while rotating, stretch with your fingertips until each piece is 30-32cm across and as thin as possible with a slightly thicker edge.

STEP 5

Sprinkle two large baking sheets with semolina and put the pizza bases on them. Top each base with the cooked onion and fennel mix, then the pieces of raw fennel, leaving a 3cm border. Drizzle with a little olive oil. Put the halved figs on top and spoon on a little balsamic vinegar and a sprinkle of sugar. Grind over some pepper. Carefully slide the first pizza onto the heated baking sheet in the oven. Bake for 8-12 mins until the dough is golden and the figs caramelised. Halfway through the cooking time, dot the pizza with the cheese. Scatter on the toasted hazelnuts and any reserved fennel fronds. Repeat with the second pizza.

Bacon & mushroom risotto

Prep:10 mins **Cook:**30 mins

Serves 4

Ingredients

- 1 tbsp olive oil
- 1 onion, chopped
- 8 rashers streaky bacon, chopped
- 250g chestnut mushroom, sliced
- 300g risotto rice
- 1l hot chicken stock
- grated parmesan, to serve

Method

STEP 1

Heat the oil in a deep frying pan and cook the onion and bacon for 5 mins to soften. Add the mushrooms and cook for a further 5 mins until they start to release their juices. Stir in the rice and cook until all the juices have been absorbed.

STEP 2

Add the stock, a ladleful at a time, stirring well and waiting for most of the stock to be absorbed before adding the next ladleful – it will take about 20 mins for all the stock to be added. Once the rice is cooked, season and serve with the grated Parmesan.

Roast aubergine parmigiana

Prep:20 mins **Cook:**1 hr and 15 mins

Serves 4

Ingredients

- 2 tbsp extra-virgin olive oil
- 2 garlic cloves , crushed
- small bunch basil , stalks finely chopped
- 2 x 400g cans cherry tomatoes
- 1 tbsp chopped sundried or semi-dried tomato
- 1 tsp clear honey
- few thyme sprigs, leaves removed
- 4 medium aubergines
- 2 balls light mozzarella , thinly sliced
- 25g breadcrumb
- 25g parmesan (or vegetarian alternative), finely grated
- crusty bread , to serve (optional)

Method

STEP 1

Heat 1 tbsp of the oil in a pan. Soften the garlic and the basil stalks for 1 min, without letting the garlic colour. Add both types of tomatoes, the honey, most of the thyme leaves and plenty of seasoning. Simmer for 5 mins – you don't want the sauce to reduce too much at this stage.

STEP 2

Meanwhile, heat oven to 200C/180C fan/gas 6. Cut 6 slits down into the flesh of each aubergine crosswise, taking care not to cut all the way through. Season inside, then push a slice of the mozzarella and a basil leaf into each gap.

STEP 3

Pour the tomato sauce into a large baking dish and sit the aubergines in it (or use 4 individual dishes). Drizzle with the remaining oil. Cover with foil and scrunch it tightly at the edges. Bake for 50 mins-1 hr until soft.

STEP 4

Remove the foil. Mix the breadcrumbs and Parmesan, and scatter over the aubergines with the rest of the thyme. Bake, uncovered, for another 15 mins or until the aubergines are very tender and the crumbs are golden and crisp. (The best way to tell if they are ready is to prod the largest aubergine in the centre with a skewer.) Let the dish rest for 5 mins, then scatter over the rest of the basil leaves. Serve with crusty bread, if you like.

Spring chicken one-pot

Prep:10 mins **Cook:**55 mins

Serves 4

Ingredients

- 1 tbsp olive oil
- 8 chicken thighs , skin on and bone in
- 1 onion , sliced
- 200g streaky bacon , chopped
- 1 carrot , chopped
- 2 large spring greens , shredded
- 600ml chicken stock
- 300g baby new potato
- 2 tbsp crème fraîche
- 2 tbsp basil pesto
- crusty bread , to serve (optional)

Method

STEP 1

Heat the oil in a large, heavy-based pan with a lid. Season the chicken and brown all over. Remove the chicken to a plate and cook the onion and bacon for 5 mins until softened and lightly coloured.

STEP 2

Return the chicken to the pan, and add the remaining ingredients, except the crème fraîche and pesto, along with plenty of freshly ground black pepper. Bring to the boil, then cover and gently simmer for 30-40 mins until the potatoes are tender and chicken cooked through.

STEP 3

Stir in the crème fraîche and pesto. Serve with some crusty bread for mopping up the sauce, if you like.

Kale pesto

Prep: 10 mins No cook

Makes enough for 10-12 servings

Ingredients

- 85g pine nut , toasted
- 85g parmesan (or vegetarian alternative), coarsely grated, plus extra to serve (optional)
- 3 garlic cloves
- 75ml extra-virgin olive oil , plus extra to serve
- 75ml olive oil
- 85g kale
- juice 1 lemon
- spaghetti or linguine, to serve

Method

STEP 1

Put the pine nuts, Parmesan, garlic, oils, kale and lemon juice in a food processor and whizz to a paste. Season to taste. Stir through hot pasta to serve, topping with extra Parmesan and olive oil, if you like.

STEP 2

To store, put in a container or jar, cover the surface with a little more olive oil and keep in the fridge for a week, or freeze for up to a month.

Lemon meringue cake

Prep:2 hrs **Cook:**1 hr

Serves 16

Ingredients

For the lemon curd

- 75g unsalted butter , softened
- 225g caster sugar
- zest 3 lemons
- 100ml lemon juice , sieved to remove any seeds and pith
- 3 large eggs
- 1 tbsp cornflour

For the caramel sugar syrup

- 85g caster sugar

For the cake

- 300g unsalted butter , softened
- 200g caster sugar
- 75g light muscovado sugar
- 300g self-raising flour
- 5 medium eggs , beaten
- 25g cornflour
- 1 tsp baking powder
- zest 4 lemons

For the caramelised lemon slices

- 1 lemon
- 175g caster sugar

For the Italian meringue

- 300g caster sugar
- 6 medium egg whites

- ½ tsp cream of tartar

Method

STEP 1

Start by making the curd. Put all the ingredients in a saucepan and whisk together. It will look like it has curdled but don't worry – simply put the pan over a low heat and stir constantly until it is smooth and thick enough to coat the back of a spoon. Pass the mixture through a sieve into a bowl. Leave to cool, covered with cling film. Put in the fridge until ready to use, preferably overnight.

STEP 2

For the caramel sugar syrup, heat the caster sugar in a saucepan over a medium heat until it melts and starts to caramelise. Stir until smooth and a deep golden colour. Remove from the heat and carefully pour in 50ml boiling water. It will steam and spit a little, so take care. (If the sugar hardens, pop the pan back on the heat for 1-2 mins to melt again.) Stir, pour immediately into a heatproof jug and top up with a little extra boiling water (about 10ml) so you have 100ml of liquid in total. Leave on one side to cool.

STEP 3

To make the cake, heat oven to 180C/160C fan/gas 4. Grease 3 x 20cm sandwich tins, lining the bases and sides with baking parchment.

STEP 4

In a large bowl, beat together the butter and sugars with an electric whisk until light and fluffy. Mix in 1 tbsp flour, then add the eggs, a little at a time, beating after each addition until fully combined.

STEP 5

Mix together the remaining dry ingredients, the lemon zest and 1/2 tsp salt, then fold in to the butter mixture with the caramel sugar syrup. Divide the batter between the tins and level the tops with the back of a wet spoon. Bake for 25-30 mins or until a skewer inserted into the middle comes out clean. Allow the cakes to cool in the tins for 10 mins, then turn out onto a wire rack, peeling off the parchment. Leave to cool completely.

STEP 6

Make the caramelised lemon slices while the cakes are baking. Slice the lemon into 5mm thick slices, discarding the ends. In a shallow non-stick pan, bring 350ml water and the sugar to the boil. Add the lemon slices, boil for 10 mins, then reduce the heat to a simmer for 20-25 mins until the liquid has evaporated and the slices have caramelised. Remove from the pan and put on a non-stick A silicone mat or baking parchment to cool.

STEP 7

To assemble the cake. Place a sponge the right way up on a cake board or presentation plate. Top with an even layer of curd but don't go right to the edge, leave about 1cm uncovered. Gently put the next sponge on top and repeat the process, putting the last sponge upside down on top.

STEP 8

To make the Italian meringue, put the sugar and 175ml water in a saucepan and B bring to a rolling boil over a high heat. Continue to boil until it reaches 115C on a sugar thermometer. Meanwhile, put the egg whites and cream of tartar in a large mixing bowl (a tabletop mixer is ideal if you have one). Whisk the egg whites to soft peaks (when lifting the whisk out, the peaks should slowly vanish back into the mixture). Whisk the egg whites at high speed and very slowly trickle in the hot syrup. The meringue will C begin to thicken and go glossy after about 10 mins. Continue to whisk until it is still just warm. Use the meringue immediately, as it is easier to work with while warm.

STEP 9

Using a palette knife, spread a thin layer of meringue around the side of the cake to level and square it up, then spread an even layer about 3mm thick on the top of the cake (see step-by-step for guidance). Put the remaining meringue in a large piping bag fitted with a small star nozzle and pipe vertical columns up the side of the cake, level with the top. Finally, pipe small meringue stars on the top of the columns. It's easier to do this with the cake on a turntable.

STEP 10

Brown the meringue using a kitchen blowtorch. Finally, cut the caramelised lemon slices in half and use to decorate the top of the cake. Will keep for 3 days in the fridge.

Ravioli with artichokes, leek & lemon

Prep: 10 mins **Cook:** 10 mins

Serves 2

Ingredients

- 280g jar artichoke antipasto, drained reserving 1 tbsp oil, artichokes roughly chopped
- 1 large leek , finely sliced
- 1 garlic clove , crushed
- 3 tbsp cream cheese
- zest and juice 1 lemon
- 250g pack spinach & ricotta ravioli
- 2 large handfuls rocket and grated Parmesan (or vegetarian alternative) to serve (optional)

Method

STEP 1

Heat the oil from the artichokes in a large saucepan, then add the leek and garlic. Fry for 5 mins over a medium heat until the leek is soft. Stir in the artichokes, cream cheese and lemon zest, then heat through. Season to taste and add a squeeze of lemon juice.

STEP 2

Meanwhile, cook the ravioli following pack instructions. Drain, add to the pan with the artichokes and cream cheese, and toss through. Serve topped with the rocket and a grating of Parmesan, if you like.

Stuffed porchetta

Prep:30 mins **Cook:**3 hrs and 5 mins plus at least 8 hrs chilling, 1 hr standing and 30 mins resting

Serves 6 - 8

Ingredients

- 1 ½kg bone-out pork belly
- 1 tbsp bicarbonate of soda
- 3 tsp fennel seeds
- 1 tsp chilli flakes

For the stuffing

- 1 tbsp extra virgin olive oil
- 1 medium onion , finely chopped
- ½ fennel bulb , hard core cut out and discarded, the rest finely chopped
- ½ tsp coriander seeds , crushed
- 2 garlic cloves , crushed
- 250g minced pork shoulder
- 1 slice sourdough bread, torn into small pieces
- 25g toasted pine nuts
- grated zest 1 unwaxed orange
- 3 dried apricots , finely chopped
- 3 sage leaves , finely chopped
- ½ tbsp rosemary leaves, chopped
- ½ tbsp lemon juice
- freshly grated nutmeg
- 1 egg , beaten

Method

STEP 1

Score the pork belly skin with a sharp knife in a cross pattern. Score down to just before where the skin meets the fat, rather than the fat itself. Bring a large saucepan of water to a simmer and add the bicarbonate of soda. Lower the pork into the water, poach gently for 5 mins, then remove it from the water and leave to cool to room temperature.

STEP 2

Meanwhile, toast the fennel seeds and chilli flakes in a dry frying pan over a high heat for 1-2 mins, then tip into a bowl and leave to cool. Grind the spices in a spice grinder or with a pestle and mortar, then mix with 1 tbsp fine sea salt.

STEP 3

Once the pork has cooled, turn it skin-side down and pierce the underside of the meat all over with a knife. Rub the meat with the spiced salt rub, cover and put it in the fridge for at least 8 hrs or overnight. Can be prepared 24 hours ahead.

STEP 4

The next day, make your stuffing. Heat the olive oil in a non-stick frying pan and add the onion and fennel. Season and cook gently over a low heat for 10 mins. Add the coriander seeds and garlic, and cook for another 2 mins, then add the mince. Cook for 8-10 mins until the mince is browned. Set aside and leave to cool.

STEP 5

Transfer the mince and onion mix to a bowl and add the sourdough, pine nuts, orange zest, apricots, herbs, lemon juice and nutmeg. Season well, then mix together thoroughly with your hands. Add the egg and mix again.

STEP 6

Lie the pork belly on a board, skin-side down. Form the stuffing into a sausage shape running all the way down the middle of the belly. Wrap the sides of the belly around the stuffing and tie with butcher's string. Place seam-side down in a roasting tin, uncovered, and chill for at least 2 hrs, preferably overnight. You want the skin to dry out completely so that it crisps up when you roast it.

STEP 7

To cook the pork, remove it from the fridge and leave it for at least 1 hr to come to room temperature before you cook it. Heat oven to 180C/160C fan/ gas 4 and cook the pork for about 2 hrs, turning the tin every 30 mins or so. After 2 hrs, turn the heat up to 220C/ 200C fan/gas 7 and cook for another 20 mins. When the pork is done, a thermometer pushed into its centre should read 77C. If the skin looks in danger of burning, cover it with foil – but only do this once it has crackled.

STEP 8

Once the pork has cooked, remove from the oven and leave to rest for 30 mins. When you're ready to carve, put the pork on a big chopping board. Using a sharp knife, slice the meat into rounds.

Sea bream in crazy water (Orata all'acqua pazza)

Prep:10 mins **Cook:**30 mins

Serves 4

Ingredients

* 4 tbsp good quality extra-virgin olive oil
* 2 whole sea bream or sea bass (about 450g each), gutted and cleaned
* 2 garlic cloves , finely sliced
* ½ small red chilli , chopped
* 400g small tomato (a mix of different-coloured cherry tomatoes would be best)
* 4 tbsp white wine
* small handful capers
* chopped parsley

Method

STEP 1

Heat half the oil in a large, lidded frying pan. Carefully slip the fish into the sizzling oil and cook for 4-5 mins until starting to brown. Flip over and scatter the garlic around the fish. Sizzle for 1 min more, then add the chilli and scatter over the tomatoes. Pour over the wine and let it bubble for 1 min, then pour over 100ml water and season generously with sea salt and pepper.

STEP 2

Put on the lid, turn up the heat and simmer for 15 mins until the fish is cooked through – you can tell when the eyes turn bright white and the flesh feels softer.

STEP 3

Lift each fish out the pan onto a serving plate and put the pan back on the heat. Add the capers and parsley, and boil hard for 1 min. You can now serve the fish and the sauce separately or slip them back into the pan, spoon some of the sauce over and bring the pan to the table. Drizzle with a little more oil just before serving.

Creamy chicken & green bean pesto pasta

Prep:10 mins **Cook:**10 mins

Serves 4

Ingredients

* 400g pasta shapes

- 250g green bean, trimmed
- 1 tbsp olive oil
- 1 bunch spring onions, finely sliced
- 2 large ready-roasted chicken breasts, shredded
- 5 tbsp pesto
- 3 tbsp double cream
- handful parmesan, grated, to serve

Method

STEP 1

Cook pasta following pack instructions, adding green beans for the final 6 mins of cooking time. Drain and reserve a few tbsps of the cooking water.

STEP 2

Meanwhile, heat olive oil in a large frying pan. Add spring onions and cook for 1-2 mins until soft, then set aside.

STEP 3

Add the shredded chicken in the pan and heat through. Stir through pesto and cream. Pop pasta and beans in with the chicken mix and stir to coat, adding a little of the cooking water. Season and sprinkle with Parmesan.

Gnocchi with courgette, mascarpone & spring onions

Prep:5 mins **Cook:**15 mins

Serves 2

Ingredients

- 300g fresh gnocchi
- 1 tbsp olive oil
- 1 red chilli , sliced, deseeded if you like
- 1 medium courgette , cut into thin ribbons with a peeler
- 4 spring onions , chopped

- zest 1 lemon
- 2 heaped tbsp mascarpone
- 50g parmesan (or vegetarian alternative), grated
- dressed mixed leaves , to serve

Method

STEP 1

Cook the gnocchi following pack instructions. Drain, reserving a ladle of the cooking water, and set aside.

STEP 2

Heat the oil in a frying pan. Cook chilli and courgette for 3 mins until soft. Add spring onions, zest, mascarpone, half the Parmesan and cooking water. Mix until smooth, add gnocchi and heat through.

STEP 3

Season, divide between 2 ovenproof dishes and scatter with the remaining Parmesan. Grill for 2-3 mins until bubbling and serve with the dressed mixed leaves.

Pancake cannelloni

Prep:30 mins **Cook:**30 mins

Serves 4

Ingredients

- 420g pack free-range pork meatballs
- 400g bag fresh spinach
- 2 tbsp basil pesto
- 250g tub ricotta
- 1 egg , beaten
- ¼ tsp ground nutmeg
- 8 pre-made pancakes
- 500g carton passata
- 1 garlic clove , crushed
- 125g ball mozzarella , torn

* 1 bunch of basil , leaves only

Method

STEP 1

Heat the grill to high and cook the meatballs for 12-15 mins on a baking tray or following pack instructions. Cut each one in half and set aside.

STEP 2

Tip the spinach into a large colander over the sink. Pour boiling water over to wilt it and leave to drain thoroughly. When cool enough to handle, squeeze out any excess liquid and chop finely. Mix the spinach with the pesto, ricotta, egg and nutmeg, then season to taste.

STEP 3

Heat oven to 190C/170C fan/gas 5. Pour the passata over the bottom of an ovenproof dish and stir in the garlic. Divide the spinach mixture between the pancakes, spreading it out in a long strip in the centre. Add meatball pieces to each one, then roll the pancake up to seal in the filling. Lay the stuffed pancakes on the passata base and top with the mozzarella. Bake for 30 mins until the cheese is melted and bubbling. Scatter over basil leaves to serve.

Gnocchi with pancetta, spinach & Parmesan cream

Total time 15 mins **Serves 4**

Ingredients

* 500g pack gnocchi
* 1 garlic clove, sliced
* 1 tbsp olive oil
* 100ml double cream
* freshly grated nutmeg
* 130g pack smoked pancetta cubes
* 100g spinach
* zest ½ lemon
* 25g parmesan, grated, plus extra for serving
* 25g toasted pine nut

Method

STEP 1

Cook the gnocchi following pack instructions, then drain. Meanwhile, heat 1 tsp of the oil in a small pan and fry the garlic, then add the cream and a good grating of nutmeg. Put to one side.

STEP 2

Heat 2 tsp of the remaining oil in a frying pan and cook the pancetta until crisp. Add the gnocchi and fry until it starts to turn golden, adding a little more oil if it begins to stick. Stir in the spinach, lemon zest and seasoning.

STEP 3

Stir the Parmesan into the cream sauce. Spoon the gnocchi onto plates, drizzle over the sauce and scatter with pine nuts. Serve with extra Parmesan.

Orange polenta cake

Prep:20 mins **Cook:**45 mins

Serves 8 - 10

Ingredients

- 250g unsalted butter
- 250g golden caster sugar
- 4 large eggs
- 140g polenta
- 200g plain flour
- 2 tsp baking powder
- zest and juice 2 oranges (less 100ml juice for the glaze)

For the orange glaze

- 100ml orange juice
- 100g golden caster sugar

Method

STEP 1

Heat oven to 160C/140C fan/gas 3. Line the base and sides of a round 23cm cake tin with baking parchment. Cream the butter and sugar together until light and fluffy. Add the eggs one at a time and mix thoroughly. Once the mixture is combined, add all the dry ingredients and the zest and juice after you have measured off 100ml for the glaze.

STEP 2

Transfer the mixture to the tin, spread evenly, then cook for about 45 mins or until a skewer inserted into the centre of the cake comes out clean. Remove from the oven and turn out onto a wire rack to cool.

STEP 3

To make the glaze, put the juice and sugar in a medium saucepan and bring to the boil. Let it simmer for 5 mins, then remove from the heat and allow to cool. Drizzle the orange glaze over the top of the cooled cake. Serve with Lemon ice cream, below.

Orecchiette with anchovies & purple sprouting broccoli

Prep:10 mins **Cook:**15 mins

Serves 2

Ingredients

- 200g orecchiette
- 4 tbsp olive oil
- 6 anchovy fillets in oil, chopped (reserve 1 tbsp oil)
- 4 fat garlic cloves , thinly sliced
- 1 red chilli , thinly sliced
- zest 1 lemon , plus juice ½
- 50g fresh breadcrumb
- 200g purple sprouting broccoli

Method

STEP 1

Cook the orecchiette following pack instructions. Meanwhile, heat 3 tbsp of the olive oil and 1 tbsp of the oil from the anchovies in a frying pan. Add the garlic and chilli, and sizzle for 3-4 mins until the garlic is just starting to turn golden. Add the anchovies and lemon juice, and cook for 1-2 mins more until the anchovies melt into the sauce. Put the remaining olive oil, breadcrumbs and lemon zest in another frying pan, stir together and cook until crisp.

STEP 2

When the pasta has 4-5 mins to go, add the broccoli to the pan. When cooked, drain, reserving a cup of the pasta water, then add to the frying pan with the garlic and anchovies. Stir and cook over a low heat for a further 2 mins, adding a splash of pasta water if it looks dry. Season, then serve in pasta bowls with the lemony crumbs sprinkled over the top.

Low-fat chicken biryani

Prep:25 mins **Cook:**1 hr and 35 mins Plus marinating

Serves 5

Ingredients

- 3 garlic cloves , finely grated
- 2 tsp finely grated ginger
- ¼ tsp ground cinnamon
- 1 tsp turmeric
- 5 tbsp natural yogurt
- 600g boneless, skinless chicken breast , cut into 4-5cm pieces
- 2 tbsp semi-skimmed milk
- good pinch saffron
- 4 medium onions
- 4 tbsp rapeseed oil
- ½ tsp hot chilli powder
- 1 cinnamon stick , broken in half
- 5 green cardamom pods , lightly bashed to split

- 3 cloves
- 1 tsp cumin seed
- 280g basmati rice
- 700ml chicken stock
- 1 tsp garam masala
- handful chopped coriander leaves

Method

STEP 1

In a mixing bowl, stir together the garlic, ginger, cinnamon, turmeric and yogurt with some pepper and ¼ tsp salt. Tip in the chicken pieces and stir to coat (see step 1, above). Cover and marinate in the fridge for about 1 hr or longer if you have time. Warm the milk to tepid, stir in the saffron and set aside.

STEP 2

Heat oven to 200C/180C fan/gas 6. Slice each onion in half lengthways, reserve half and cut the other half into thin slices. Pour 1½ tbsp of the oil onto a baking tray, scatter over the sliced onion, toss to coat, then spread out in a thin, even layer (step 2). Roast for 40-45 mins, stirring halfway, until golden.

STEP 3

When the chicken has marinated, thinly slice the reserved onion. Heat 1 tbsp oil in a large sauté or frying pan. Fry the onion for 4-5 mins until golden. Stir in the chicken, a spoonful at a time, frying until it is no longer opaque, before adding the next spoonful (this helps to prevent the yogurt from curdling). Once the last of the chicken has been added, stir-fry for a further 5 mins until everything looks juicy. Scrape any sticky bits off the bottom of the pan, stir in the chilli powder, then pour in 100ml water, cover and simmer on a low heat for 15 mins. Remove and set aside.

STEP 4

Cook the rice while the chicken simmers. Heat another 1 tbsp oil in a large sauté pan, then drop in the cinnamon stick, cardamom, cloves and cumin seeds. Fry briefly until their aroma is released. Tip in the rice (step 3) and fry for 1 min, stirring constantly. Stir in the stock and bring to the boil. Lower the heat and simmer, covered, for about 8 mins or until all the stock has been absorbed. Remove from the heat and leave with the lid on for a few mins, so the rice can fluff up. Stir the garam masala into the remaining 1½ tsp oil and set aside. When the onions are roasted, remove and reduce oven to 180C/160C fan/gas 4.

STEP 5

Spoon half the chicken and its juices into an ovenproof dish, about 25 x 18 x 6cm, then scatter over a third of the roasted onions. Remove the whole spices from the rice, then layer half of the rice over the chicken and onions. Drizzle over the spiced oil. Spoon over the rest of the chicken and a third more onions. Top with the remaining rice (step 4) and drizzle over the saffron-infused milk. Scatter over the rest of the onions, cover tightly with foil and heat through in the oven for about 25 mins. Serve scattered with the mint and coriander.

Spicy meatballs with chilli black beans

Prep:20 mins **Cook:**25 mins

Serves 4

Ingredients

- 1 red onion, halved and sliced
- 2 garlic cloves, sliced
- 1 large yellow pepper, quartered, deseeded and diced
- 1 tsp ground cumin
- 2-3 tsp chipotle chilli paste
- 300ml reduced-salt chicken stock
- 400g can cherry tomatoes
- 400g can black beans or red kidney beans, drained
- 1 avocado, stoned, peeled and chopped
- juice ½ lime

For the meatballs

- 500g pack turkey breast mince
- 50g porridge oats
- 2 spring onions, finely chopped
- 1 tsp ground cumin
- 1 tsp coriander
- small bunch coriander, chopped, stalks and leaves kept separate

- 1 tsp rapeseed oil

Method

STEP 1

First make the meatballs. Tip the mince into a bowl, add the oats, spring onions, spices and the coriander stalks, then lightly knead the ingredients together until well mixed. Shape into 12 ping-pong- sized balls. Heat the oil in a non-stick frying pan, add the meatballs and cook, turning them frequently, until golden. Remove from the pan.

STEP 2

Tip the onion and garlic into the pan with the pepper and stir-fry until softened. Stir in the cumin and chilli paste, then pour in the stock. Return the meatballs to the pan and cook, covered, over a low heat for 10 mins. Stir in the tomatoes and beans, and cook, uncovered, for a few mins more. Toss the avocado chunks in the lime juice and serve the meatballs topped with the avocado and coriander leaves.

Slow cooker shepherd's pie

Prep:1 hr **Cook:**5 hrs

Serves 4

Ingredients

- 1 tbsp olive oil
- 1 onion, finely chopped
- 3-4 thyme sprigs
- 2 carrots, finely diced
- 250g lean (10%) mince lamb or beef
- 1 tbsp plain flour
- 1 tbsp tomato purée
- 400g can lentils, or white beans
- 1 tsp Worcestershire sauce

For the topping

- 650g potatoes, peeled and cut into chunks
- 250g sweet potatoes, peeled and cut into chunks

- 2 tbsp half-fat crème fraîche

Method

STEP 1

Heat the slow cooker if necessary. Heat the oil in a large frying pan. Tip the onions and thyme sprigs and fry for 2-3 mins. Then add the carrots and fry together, stirring occasionally until the vegetables start to brown. Stir in the mince and fry for 1-2 mins until no longer pink. Stir in the flour then cook for another 1-2 mins. Stir in the tomato purée and lentils and season with pepper and the Worcestershire sauce, adding a splash of water if you think the mixture is too dry. Scrape everything into the slow cooker.

STEP 2

Meanwhile cook both lots of potatoes in simmering water for 12-13 minutes or until they are cooked through. Drain well and then mash with the crème fraîche. Spoon this on top of the mince mixture and cook on Low for 5 hours - the mixture should be bubbling at the sides when it is ready. Crisp up the potato topping under the grill if you like.

Curried spinach, eggs & chickpeas

Prep:15 mins **Cook:**35 mins

Serves 2

Ingredients

- 1 tbsp rapeseed oil
- 1 onion , thinly sliced
- 1 garlic clove , crushed
- 3cm piece ginger , peeled and grated
- 1 tsp ground turmeric
- 1 tsp ground coriander
- 1 tsp garam masala
- 1 tbsp ground cumin
- 450g tomatoes , chopped
- 400g can chickpeas , drained
- 1 tsp sugar
- 200g spinach

- 2 large eggs
- 3 tbsp natural yogurt
- 1 red chilli , finely sliced
- ½ small bunch of coriander , torn

Method

STEP 1

Heat the oil in a large frying pan or flameproof casserole pot over a medium heat, and fry the onion for 10 mins until golden and sticky. Add the garlic, ginger, turmeric, ground coriander, garam masala, cumin and tomatoes, and fry for 2 mins more. Add the chickpeas, 100ml water and the sugar and bring to a simmer. Stir in the spinach, then cover and cook for 20-25 mins. Season to taste.

STEP 2

Cook the eggs in a pan of boiling water for 7 mins, then rinse under cold running water to cool. Drain, peel and halve. Swirl the yogurt into the curry, then top with the eggs, chilli and coriander. Season.

Cabbage soup

Prep:20 mins **Cook:**50 mins

Serves 6

Ingredients

- 2 tbsp olive oil
- 1 large onion , finely chopped
- 2 celery sticks , finely chopped
- 1 large carrot , finely chopped
- 70g smoked pancetta , diced (optional)
- 1 large Savoy cabbage , shredded
- 2 fat garlic cloves , crushed
- 1 heaped tsp sweet smoked paprika
- 1 tbsp finely chopped rosemary
- 1 x 400g can chopped tomatoes
- 1.7l hot vegetable stock

- 1 x 400g can chickpeas , drained and rinsed
- shaved parmesan (or vegetarian alternative), to serve (optional)
- crusty bread , to serve (optional)

Method

STEP 1

Heat the oil in a casserole pot over a low heat. Add the onion, celery and carrot, along with a generous pinch of salt, and fry gently for 15 mins, or until the veg begins to soften. If you're using pancetta, add it to the pan, turn up the heat and fry for a few mins more until turning golden brown. Tip in the cabbage and fry for 5 mins, then stir through the garlic, paprika and rosemary and cook for 1 min more.

STEP 2

Tip the chopped tomatoes and stock into the pan. Bring to a simmer, then cook, uncovered, for 30 mins, adding the chickpeas for the final 10 mins. Season generously with salt and black pepper.

STEP 3

Ladle the soup into six deep bowls. Serve with the shaved parmesan and crusty bread, if you like.

Red pepper, squash & harissa soup

Prep:15 mins **Cook:**1 hr

Serves 6

Ingredients

- 1 small butternut squash (about 600-700g), peeled and cut into chunks
- 2 red pepper , roughly chopped
- 2 red onion , roughly chopped
- 3 tbsp rapeseed oil
- 3 garlic cloves in their skins
- 1 tbsp ground coriander
- 2 tsp ground cumin
- 1.2l chicken or vegetable stock

- 2 tbsp harissa paste
- 50ml double cream

Method

STEP 1

Heat oven to 180C/160C fan/gas 4. Put all the veg on a large baking tray and toss together with rapeseed oil, garlic cloves in their skins, ground coriander, ground cumin and some seasoning. Roast for 45 mins, moving the veg around in the tray after 30 mins, until soft and starting to caramelise. Squeeze the garlic cloves out of their skins. Tip everything into a large pan. Add the chicken or vegetable stock, harissa paste and double cream. Bring to a simmer and bubble for a few mins. Blitz the soup in a blender, check the seasoning and add more liquid if you need to. Serve swirled with extra cream and harissa.

Warm cherry & brown sugar compote

Prep:5 mins **Cook:**15 mins

Serves 4

Ingredients

- 390g jar cherries in kirsch
- 2 tbsp dark brown sugar
- 4 big scoops of vanilla ice cream
- 50g amaretti biscuits

Method

STEP 1

Tip the cherries and sugar into a small saucepan. Bring to a simmer over a medium heat, stirring, and allow to bubble for 10 mins. Leave to cool slightly.

STEP 2

Scoop the ice cream into four bowls and pour over the warm compote. Crumble over the amaretti and serve.

Harissa-crumbed fish with lentils & peppers

Prep:15 mins **Cook:**15 mins

Serves 4

Ingredients

- 2 x 200g pouches cooked puy lentils
- 200g jar roasted red peppers , drained and torn into chunks
- 50g black olives , from a jar, roughly chopped
- 1 lemon , zested and cut into wedges
- 3 tbsp olive or rapeseed oil
- 4 x 140g cod fillets (or another white fish)
- 100g fresh breadcrumbs
- 1 tbsp harissa
- ½ small pack flat-leaf parsley , chopped

Method

STEP 1

Heat oven to 200C/180C fan/gas 6. Mix the lentils, peppers, olives, lemon zest, 2 tbsp oil and some seasoning in a roasting tin. Top with the fish fillets. Mix the breadcrumbs, harissa and the remaining oil and put a few spoonfuls on top of each piece of fish. Bake for 12-15 mins until the fish is cooked, the topping is crispy and the lentils are hot. Scatter with the parsley and squeeze over the lemon wedges.

Crispy Asian salmon with stir-fried noodles, pak choi & sugar snap peas

Prep:10 mins **Cook:**15 mins

Serves 2

Ingredients

- 2 x 100g salmon fillets (plus 2 more 100g salmon fillets if cooking for Flaked salmon salad lunch - see 'goes well with')
- For the marinade

- 2 tsp reduced salt tamari or soy sauce
- 2cm piece ginger, peeled and finely chopped or grated
- 1 garlic clove, finely chopped
- 2 tbsp lemon or lime juice
- 1 tsp sesame oil
- For the stir-fried noodles
- 85g vermicelli rice noodle
- 2 tsp rapeseed oil
- 1 tsp sesame oil
- 1 spring onion, trimmed and thinly sliced
- 1 garlic clove, finely chopped
- ½ red chilli, deseeded and finely chopped
- 2cm piece ginger, peeled and finely chopped
- 100g sugar snap pea
- 100g pak choi (or spinach)
- 1 large red pepper, sliced
- 1 tsp tamari or soy sauce
- 1 tsp Thai fish sauce
- juice ½ lime
- 1 tbsp finely chopped coriander

Method

STEP 1

Make the marinade by mixing together all the ingredients. Place the salmon fillets in a small bowl and spoon over the marinade, turning the fish so that it's nicely coated. Cover with cling film and leave to sit for 10 mins (or longer if you have time).

STEP 2

Meanwhile, cook the noodles following pack instructions, then drain and sit them in a bowl of cold water.

STEP 3

Heat a non-stick frying pan. Add the salmon fillets, skin-side down, and leave for 3 mins. When the fish is slightly crispy, flip over and cook for a further 3 mins on the other side. Just before you remove the fish from the pan, add any remaining marinade and let it sizzle for 10 secs.

Place 2 of the fillets, skin-side up, with their juices on a plate and cover with foil to keep warm. Put the other 2 fillets on another plate if using for Flaked salmon salad (see 'goes well with'), cover with foil, leave to cool, then chill.

STEP 4

In a frying pan or wok, heat the rapeseed and sesame oils over a high heat. Add the spring onion, garlic, chilli and ginger, and stir constantly for about 1 min. Add the sugar snap peas, pak choi and pepper, and stir for another 1-2 mins, then add the cooked noodles. Toss well, then add the soy sauce, fish sauce and lime juice, and mix until well combined and the pan is sizzling.

STEP 5

Remove from the heat and divide between 2 bowls. Top each with a salmon fillet and drizzle over any juices. Sprinkle with coriander and serve.

Turkey meatloaf

Prep:15 mins **Cook:**55 mins

Serves 4

Ingredients

- 1 tbsp olive oil
- 1 large onion , finely chopped
- 1 garlic clove , crushed
- 2 tbsp Worcestershire sauce
- 2 tsp tomato purée , plus 1 tbsp for the beans
- 500g turkey mince (thigh is best)
- 1 large egg , beaten
- 85g fresh white breadcrumbs
- 2 tbsp barbecue sauce , plus 4 tbsp for the beans
- 2 x 400g cans cannellini beans
- 1-2 tbsp roughly chopped parsley

Method

STEP 1

Heat oven to 180C/160C fan/gas 4. Heat the oil in a large frying pan and cook the onion for 8-10 mins until softened. Add the garlic, Worcestershire sauce and 2 tsp tomato purée, and stir until combined. Set aside to cool.

STEP 2

Put the turkey mince, egg, breadcrumbs and cooled onion mix in a large bowl and season well. Mix everything to combine, then shape into a rectangular loaf and place in a large roasting tin. Spread 2 tbsp barbecue sauce over the meatloaf and bake for 30 mins.

STEP 3

Meanwhile, drain 1 can of beans only, then pour both cans into a large bowl. Add the remaining barbecue sauce and tomato purée. Season and set aside.

STEP 4

When the meatloaf has had its initial cooking time, scatter the beans around the outside and bake for 15 mins more until the meatloaf is cooked through and the beans are piping hot. Scatter over the parsley and serve the meatloaf in slices.

Ginger, sesame and chilli prawn & broccoli stir-fry

Prep:5 mins **Cook:**10 mins

Serves 2

Ingredients

- 250g broccoli , thin-stemmed if you like, cut into even-sized florets
- 2 balls stem ginger , finely chopped, plus 2 tbsp syrup from the jar
- 3 tbsp low-salt soy sauce
- 1 garlic clove , crushed
- 1 red chilli , a little thinly sliced, the rest deseeded and finely chopped
- 2 tsp sesame seeds
- ½ tbsp sesame oil
- 200g raw king prawns
- 100g beansprouts
- cooked rice or noodles, to serve

Method

STEP 1

Heat a pan of water until boiling. Tip in the broccoli and cook for just 1 min – it should still have a good crunch. Meanwhile, mix the stem ginger and syrup, soy sauce, garlic and finely chopped chilli.

STEP 2

Toast the sesame seeds in a dry wok or large frying pan. When they're nicely browned, turn up the heat and add the oil, prawns and cooked broccoli. Stir-fry for a few mins until the prawns turn pink. Pour over the ginger sauce, then tip in the beansprouts. Cook for 30 seconds, or until the beansprouts are heated thoroughly, adding a splash more soy or ginger syrup, if you like. Scatter with the sliced chilli and serve over rice or noodles.

Paneer jalfrezi with cumin rice

Prep:20 mins **Cook:**30 mins

Serves 4

Ingredients

- 2 tsp cold-pressed rapeseed oil
- 1 large and 1 medium onion , large one finely chopped and medium one cut into wedges
- 2 large garlic cloves , chopped
- 50g ginger , peeled and shredded
- 2 tsp ground coriander
- 2 tsp cumin seeds
- 400g can chopped tomatoes
- 1 tbsp vegetable bouillon powder
- 135g paneer , chopped
- 2 large peppers , seeded and chopped
- 1 red or green chilli , deseeded and sliced
- 25g coriander , chopped

For the rice

- 260g brown basmati rice
- 1 tsp cumin seeds

Method

STEP 1

Heat 1 tsp oil a large non-stick frying pan and fry the chopped onions, garlic and half the ginger for 5 mins until softened. Add the ground coriander and cumin seeds and cook for 1 min more, then tip in the tomatoes, half a can of water and the bouillon. Blitz everything together with a stick blender until very smooth, then bring to a simmer. Cover and cook for 15 mins.

STEP 2

Meanwhile, cook the rice and cumin seeds in a pan of boiling water for 25 mins, or until tender.

STEP 3

Heat the remaining oil in a non-stick wok and fry the paneer until lightly coloured. Remove from the pan and set aside. Add the peppers, onion wedges and chilli to the pan and stir-fry until the veg is tender, but still retains some bite. Mix the stir-fried veg and paneer into the sauce with the chopped coriander, then serve with the rice. If you're following our Healthy Diet Plan, eat two portions of the curry and rice, then chill the rest for another day. Will keep for up to three days, covered, in the fridge. To serve on the second night, reheat the leftover portions in the microwave until piping hot.

Low 'n' slow rib steak with Cuban mojo salsa

Prep:20 mins **Cook:**3 hrs and 20 mins

Serves 2

Ingredients

- 1 rib steak on the bone or côte du boeuf (about 800g)
- 1 tbsp rapeseed oil
- 1 garlic clove
- 2 thyme sprigs
- 25g butter , chopped into small pieces
- sweet potato fries
- a dressed salad , to serve

For the mojo salsa

- 2 limes
- 1 small orange
- ½ small bunch mint , finely chopped
- small bunch coriander , finely chopped
- 4 spring onions , finely chopped
- 1 small garlic clove , crushed
- 1 fat green chilli , finely chopped
- 4 tbsp extra virgin rapeseed oil or olive oil

Method

STEP 1

Leave the beef at room temperature for about 1 hr before you cook it. Heat oven to 60C/40C fan/gas 1 /4 if you like your beef medium rare, or 65C/45C fan/gas 1 /4 for medium. (Cooking at these low temperatures will be more accurate in an electric oven than in a gas one. If using gas, put the oven on the lowest setting you have, and be aware that the cooking time may be shorter.)

STEP 2

Put the unseasoned beef in a heavy-based ovenproof frying pan. Cook in the middle of the oven for 3 hrs undisturbed.

STEP 3

Meanwhile, make the salsa. Zest the limes and orange into a bowl. Cut each in half and place, cut-side down, in a hot pan. Cook for a few mins until the fruits are charred, then squeeze the juice into the bowl. Add the other ingredients and season well.

STEP 4

When the beef is cooked, it should look dry on the surface, and dark pink in colour. If you have a meat thermometer, test the internal temperature – it should be 58-60C. Remove the pan from the oven and set over a high heat on the hob. Add the oil and sear the meat on both sides for a few mins until caramelised. Sear the fat for a few mins too. Smash the garlic clove with the heel of your hand and add this to the pan with the thyme and butter. When the butter is foaming, spoon it over the beef and cook for another 1-2 mins. Transfer the beef to a warm plate, cover with foil, and leave to rest for 5-10 mins. Carve away from the bone and into slices before serving with the salsa, fries and salad.